A *Leck* in th'*Ear*

Anne Morrin

Trafford
PUBLISHING

 www.trafford.com

North America & international
toll-free: 1 888 232 4444 (USA & Canada)
phone: 250 383 6864 ♦ fax: 250 383 6804 ♦ email: info@trafford.com

The United Kingdom & Europe
phone: +44 (0)1865 722 113 ♦ local rate: 0845 230 9601
facsimile: +44 (0)1865 722 868 ♦ email: info.uk@trafford.com

10 9 8 7 6 5 4 3 2

ACKNOWLEDGEMENTS

Proof Reading: *Kay Morrin*
                      Elizabeth Morrin
Cover and Design: *Claire Morrin*

3

CHAPTER I

The Green Years

I remember as a youngster standing on the summit of Dans
Hill where I had a panoramic view of the surrounding
countryside and thinking, "Isn't the world a huge place".
To me, the world was what I could see from where I
stood, with the Twelve Pins and Mount Gable far away in the
distance marking the end of it all.

The long stretch of sun-dappled Lough Corrib which
was clearly visible on the horizon confirmed my belief that
the world ended there. After all, a huge swell of lake-water
seemed to be heaving relentlessly against the rugged rocky
mountains, and in turn, the mountains appeared to climb
endlessly into a cloudless azure sky. There was no way that
anyone or anything could venture beyond that impossible
barrier.

When I reached the top of the next hill I could, and
usually did, scramble on to the pillar of the old iron gate
and look down on the village nestling comfortably in the
hollow below. The volume and consistency of the smoke
spiralling from the chimneys of the houses beneath me was
an indication of the progress - or lack of it - that was made
in the homes while we children were at school all day. Thick
dark-blue smoke curling vigorously skywards signaled that
turf had just been added to hitherto dying embers, and dinner
in the three-legged pot was about to be suspended above the
fire to boil.

We preferred to see lazy plumes of almost invisible grey
smoke trickling languidly downwards, indicating that the

5

burning turf was a mass of red hot coals and the traditional feed of bacon and cabbage, boiling for some time, was well-nigh on its way to the table.

I secretly wondered if my father was reading the "smoke signals" as accurately as we did. He always managed to walk in from the fields at the precise moment that my mother was taking the bacon from the pot. He rarely had to be called, despite having a whistle left on the middle shelf of the dresser specially for that purpose. His timely arrival averted numerous rows as each sibling hoped to be the chosen one to perform this important task - not that we had any particular wish to call him to his dinner - but one of us would delight in blasting the eardrums off the irate losers with that awful shrill piercing sound.

To this day, I cannot understand how we youngsters were capable of tucking into such heavy meals every afternoon, particularly in autumn when we were full to the gills with crab-apples and blackberries devoured by the handful on our way home from school. Perhaps the certainty that there would be nothing else on offer had a definite influence on our willingness to gulp down every morsel before we scampered outside for the evening.

I was one of a large family, which is not surprising, considering that big families were prevalent in the thirties and forties. Family planning was unheard of then, and would not, in any case, be tolerated by the church. Women were bound by catholicism to live with their husbands as "sister and brother" if for reasons of ill-health or otherwise they avoided another pregnancy.

The reproductive drive, undoubtedly one of our strongest instinctive urges, was not only encouraged by "fire and brimstone" sermons from the altar every Sunday, but also, conversely, restricted by those same sermons. Any couple who engaged in this "sinful", albeit natural act, for anything other than procreation was damned in hell forever.

"Have plenty of them. They are God's grandest flowers", the parish priest commanded at full volume, and while most of the young mothers agreed that their children were indeed "God's grandest flowers", they had serious reservations as to their ability to cope with the output His Reverence expected of them. It was not unusual to have two babies still in nappies when a third arrived on the scene. But those dutiful mothers managed somehow to get through the trials and tribulations - not to mention the continuous tubs of washing - firmly believing they were putting their purgatory over them.

I have abiding memories of a good friend and relation of my mother coming to visit after one particularly difficult birth. She tucked one shilling into the new-born baby's fist and whispered,

"It's all I have Mary", apologising for the small amount. It might not have been much - very true- but the memory of a warm, loving, generous woman with ten children of her own, who could ill afford to favour us with gifts, however small, has remained with me all my life. Those wonderful women were the salt of the earth. I am reminded of them today when the TV ad. asks,

"Do you love someone enough to give them your last Rolo?"

They most certainly did.

Many years later it was astonishing to learn that there were at least two women in the parish who, on advice passed down to them from their own mothers, engaged in a form of contraception by swallowing copious potions of Glauber Salts on the morning-after-the-night-before. While it was not always successful it certainly was a help they maintained. As one of these ladies put it on telling the story in her old age,

"God bless the Glauber Salts. Only for it I'd have doubled the number".

She already had thirteen children.

Those women told their secret to no one. Not to their husbands and certainly not to their confessor who would refuse absolution in the confessional and threaten them with a journey to Tuam to obtain the Bishop's pardon which they were unlikely to be granted for such an "awful sin".

The feeling of "wrong-doing" and "mortal sin" persisted and played on their conscience to the extent that they were convinced the Lord would punish them in His anger by sending them deformed or retarded babies next time round. Nothing like that happened, of course. Healthy bouncing babies continued to arrive until Old Mother Nature decided to intervene, sometimes belatedly, despite urgent prayers and aspirations to the contrary.

Thoughts linger in my memory of the year our twins were born. For weeks before a baby's birth my mother had the assiduous task of fashioning tiny garments for the new-comer, and this year was no exception. At this particular time she went on her annual shopping "spree" to McCormacks in Ballinrobe to purchase all her requirements for the big sewing session.

Such was the service in this select establishment that if my mother was indisposed she wrote out a list which my father duly presented to the head salesman when he went to town on fair-day-Monday.

Having studied the list carefully the salesman always suggested that my father return in an hour, by which time he had the baby cloth cut out and neatly packaged. He rarely made errors. The mothers-to-be trusted him completely. He wasn't just a great salesman. He was a "ladies man" in the nicest possible way. Such manners. Such courtesy. Such a feeling of being his very special customer. That man could coax the birds off the trees with his smooth-talking ways. He guided his customers to the far end of the long counter to talk privately and advise them that "swansdown" or "winceyette" was soon going to be in short supply. Not surprisingly, Tim always managed to sell them a little bit more than they intended to purchase, but he knew just as well as the women did, that the extra yard would "never go to loss".

My mother was both shocked and surprised when she was delivered of two babies that autumn. Such a thought never entered her head beforehand. The doctor said later that he "suspected" she was carrying twins which was not strictly correct as he had no contact with her during her pregnancy. Expectant mothers did not visit their GP in those days unless there was something seriously wrong. They sent their husbands instead to "book" him for the big event.

As youngsters we knew without a word being said that we were about to get a new baby when my father got on his bike in his good jacket, on a weekday, and pedalled three miles to "call" the doctor. That important man always rushed in our front door carrying a black bag and headed straight for the bedroom where my mother was at an advanced stage of labour. We knew why he was practically running. The baby would smother if he wasn't taken out of the black bag quickly. We had seen it all year after year. But his time, to our amazement, the doctor was carrying two bags and we whispered to each other,

"We're going to get two this time".

In actual fact, the second bag contained nothing more than eighteen huge apples for my father. Apparently on the night he went to "book" the G.P. they talked about some new variety of apple which the doctor had in his garden, and eager to brag a little, he brought with him eighteen of the finest apples ever seen in our locality.

It was such a let-down for us children, but three hours later when we could actually hear two babies bawling simultaneously, our deepest suspicions were aroused. That doctor must have packed the two babies into one bag and the apples into the second bag, we decided. We were loud in our condemnation for days afterwards.

The doctor seemed to take forever to gather up his bags and leave. We waited impatiently to get a glimpse of the newborns, but did not dare approach the room door. He sat at the kitchen table with my father discussing the 1916 Rising and the Irish Volunteers, while in the bedroom my mother struggled in vain to hide the tears, and prayed to God to get her through the next few years.

Without Him she simply could not cope.

How could Doctor Ned say he "suspected" twins, she wondered, when she had never contacted him during her pregnancy? Not that she would ever hold it against him. He was her Saviour. In fact, he was the Saviour of all women in the locality.

"He never lost a baby yet", they bragged, as if it were he who gave birth.

Never, ever would it be attributed to their own excellent health or sheer good luck.

As usual, my grandmother came to help out. We knew my father would be putting the horse under the side-car to fetch her, and as usual there was a row about who would accompany him and who would stay at home. Always short-tempered under pressure, he invariably left the lot of us looking forlorn while he drove away down the road alone.

He returned within the hour with Grandma who looked displeased and unhappy. She was peevish with all of us that evening and we avoided her for most of the time. She certainly had not expected to hear of the twins arrival and went about her work with a worried look on her face.

In one of her good moments she allowed me to hold one of the babies while she attended to the needs of the other. Curiosity overcame me and just as I peeped inside the blanket at the sleeping infant, Grandma delivered a stinging leck in

10

th'ear and warned me I'd know "What's what" if I let the child fall. The back of Grandma's bony hand left its mark on my skinny little cheek for hours.

At the end of nine days when my mother was allowed out of bed, Grandma couldn't wait to get back to the peace and quiet of her own home.

"See that the oldest ones mind the twins" she snapped, looking directly at me.

Then she whispered to my mother, "I hope this is the last of them. How in God's name are you going to manage at all, at all."

But manage my mother did. It was comforting to have her in the kitchen again. We could not understand why she suddenly took to the bed, and could only assume she was minding the new babies. We looked in admiration at our much slimmer mother, having no idea why she lost her "belly", but for all our naiveté we instinctively knew she possessed that certain something, that only mothers have, to make a house feel like a real home.

The old Iron Gate.

CHAPTER 2

Grandma

We were never too enamoured with Grandma's annual visits. She was a spirited woman who commanded respect at all times. She seemed so haughty and remote when she dressed up in her black cape and bonnet for Sunday Mass that we almost feared her. But that fear abated somewhat when she slipped into the familiar red petticoat and long black skirt the moment she arrived in from Mass.

She detested wet Sundays. The rain flattened the feathers on her bonnet, and we watched fascinated, while she threw a fist of salt into the fire and waited until it sparked and crackled. Holding the bonnet close to the sparks, she twisted and turned it until the feathers dried out and resumed their normal appearance. Much attention was given to the extra long feathers on the side of the bonnet to ensure they stood erect, with the tips bending over gracefully like the branches of a weeping willow.

When she bade good-morning to other church-goers she inclined her head slightly to hear what they had to say, then she drew herself up and the long feathers dipped and danced with each other atop of her silver grey hair. It was then she looked every inch of the imperious dowager who was not Grandma but some stranger from another world.

We were more than a little relieved when she put her finery away and donned the familiar week-day garb. There were some anxious seconds as she patted her pockets. It would be a "bad job" for anyone who was sorely tempted to raid her apron pocket in her absence for the few hot sweets she kept there for her own personal use. Although we were aware of their nasty burning taste, we still managed to look hard-done-by when she popped one into her mouth.

"Sweets are bad for 'childher'", she cautioned with a lecture on the damaging effects sweets had on the teeth, and wagging her finger knowingly she continued,

"There is nothing so disgusting as a mouthful of rotted teeth".

We looked at her own toothless grin and wondered.

Our parents fully supported her, we soon realised. A neighbouring woman called occasionally for my father when his assistance was required to bring bags of grain up to the loft in the local mill. She usually brought a "penn'erth" of 'can sweets' for us children, but we had to remember our teeth, and the sweets were stored away for my aunt who came to help out with the washing on Wednesdays.

Grandma didn't entirely approve of the amount of time her son-in-law spent 'working for nothing' in the mill - even though it was a night-time task solely to help out a neighbour, and something he enjoyed immensely. But Grandma could think of other things awaiting his attention, like putting heels and toe-caps on our shoes.

She must have said as much at some stage, because we once heard him snap at my mother and say,

"She's like a cock on a dung-hill watching everyone".

Needless to say, my mother was none too pleased with such an uncomplimentary remark about Grandma. We could feel the chill in the air for hours afterwards.

Although we were not fully aware of the reasons, we youngsters shared a certain empathy with our father. Nothing escaped Grandma's crafty eyes. But with the passing of time we realised she needed all her wits about her to cope with such an unruly lot.

"I know every trick in the book", she was wont to say. "Ye might be able to fool ye're mother, but ye won't fool me". Most times she softened it with a smile that clearly said "Don't try on anything", and gave us an apple if we kept out of mischief for awhile.

Once after a particularly trying day she sat on a stool near the fire and allowed three of us - two on her lap and one behind her - to comb and re-comb her silver tresses. Nothing could compare then with the magic of watching all the waves settling back into her hair while we practically scraped her scalp off. She squeezed her eyes and grimaced and endured it all before shooing us away with,

"Off ye go now to the well for a can o' wather and DONT DELAY".

Her dearest wish was to see the "makings" of a priest emerge from our prolific family. She had already chosen her own man of the cloth. Four-year old Bobby, the only fair-haired boy among the brothers, was selected for this ecclesiastical honour for his angelic looks and his "quieter-than-the-rest-of-them" disposition.

She petted and spoiled him, causing resentment among the older boys. Not because he might be a priest one day, but for the fact that he was allowed to share her mug of tea and half of her Gearys currant biscuit....... her one little luxury when the family was fed and sent to the garden to play. Alas for Grandma, celibacy did not enter into his scheme of things as manhood approached. Bobby had met and married the love of his life at the age of twenty-two.

Christenings were very low-key events in our youth, emphasizing the religious aspect only. Baby was taken to the church to be cleansed of original sin regardless of weather conditions when he or she was three or four days old. The old people proudly boasted that a baby never got a cold when he was baptised, perhaps for the very good reason that he was practically smothered in christening shawl and blankets.

14

Grandma was godmother to at least five of us over the years, and on each occasion one of her sons stepped into the role of godfather with her. We watched her scrubbing her face with buttermilk beforehand, and were told that she must stand before God and make a solemn promise to see that the baby was brought up in the Catholic religion, therefore she had to be squeaky clean to meet the Lord and do His bidding. There were no celebrations afterwards apart from a much needed cup of tea. Normal work resumed almost immediately.

One wonders what the grandparents of yesteryear would think of today's christenings with little or no emphasis on religion and all thoughts on new outfits for the entire family, with a five-course meal in a Grade A hotel afterwards.

Today the priest is dazzled with flash-bulbs during the short baptismal ceremony and camcorders are busy recording every move....from 'junior' trying to climb on to the altar to cousin Martha who has flown home from Australia especially for this day. Names of rock stars and film stars have taken over from the saints of Ireland and the Mary Annes and Bridgets and Michaels are gradually fading into obscurity.

Memories abound of a christening when two next door neighbours were God parents to a new arrival in our house. We were on our way home from school when my father drove by with the horse and side-car carrying the christening 'party' to the church.

Our golden opportunity! Nothing could compare with the excitement of having the whole evening to ourselves without supervision, totally heedless of the fact that Grandma was at home watching the clock.

We sauntered in to the forge on the roadside and watched in admiration as Grehan, the black-smith, put shoes on a horse, while another horse stood outside the door awaiting his turn. We fought over who would blow the bellows on the already roaring coal fire until Grehan told us to "clear off to

Hell". We didn't, of course. We knew he'd soon forget if we stopped fighting, and so mind-boggling was the blacksmiths difficult task of nailing red-hot shoes to the horses' hooves that we lost all sense of time until ..... horror of horrors..... the side-car and its occupants were passing by once more on the return journey from the church. We scampered after them, hoping, rather naively, to slip through unnoticed while baby was taken indoors, but our luck had run out. Grandma was waiting with the sally rod in her hand, partly hidden in the folds of her apron, and we set forth to school next morning with big angry-looking weals across the backs of our legs. Perhaps we could have got off lighter if we had not insisted that we simply wanted to warm our hands at the big coal fire in the forge.

"It was freezing outside", we maintained with a great display of innocence.

"On a hot day in the month of June?" Grandma snorted. "Ye must think I was hatched out yesterday". We had less credibility than ever before following that incident.

Little did we realise it then, the day Grandma returned to her own home when the twins were nine days old, that we would never again see her in our house. She suffered a severe stroke some months later and was confined to her bed and her armchair for the remainder of her life.

My sister and I were sent to visit her once a week and were told to watch carefully "to see if she knows ye". She did. Usually after a painfully slow struggle she managed to jerk out the words,

"How're the ladeens?"

My mother missed her unbearably fourteen months later when the last of her children was born. For the first time in her life she was hospitalized after giving birth, and relations expressed much concern that baby was left in the hands of the oldest girl....... then a twelve year old. Very capable hands they proved to be, to everyone's surprise. She rose to the occasion with admirable wisdom... far beyond her years, equalling any mother protecting her young, and refusing to part with her, even for one day.

Getting out of bed in the middle of the night to heat up milk for baby's feeds began to take its toll, most notably when my sister, with baby in her arms, dropped off to sleep from sheer fatigue, and woke only when my father charged down to the kitchen to castigate whoever was "burnin' candles at this hour o' the night".

Never one for baby-feeding or household chores, he found my mother's absence quite alarming and took himself off to bed, muttering,

"She won't come back a minit too soon", as if that explained the "burning of the midnight oil".

Grandma died soon afterwards. My sister and I were on our weekly visit when she passed away, and we hung around while my uncle found a scarf to wrap round her head and keep her prayer-book firmly in place beneath her chin until rigor mortis set in.

She lay on her bed dressed in a long brown "habit" that did nothing for her colouring, with her rosary beads entwined round her fingers. Three lighted candles stood on a table at her bedside and the more we looked the more nervous we became, until we convinced ourselves she had changed into an old man with a wrinkled weather-beaten face.

In keeping with some time-honoured tradition my uncle removed her feather pillows from beneath her head, and filled up the pillow-cases with new mown hay. While hay usually smells good outdoors, it was quite overpowering in the small airless room. Added to which was the pungent odour from a huge bunch of Lily-of-the-Valley and the warm waxy fumes from the blessed candles.

A truly unimaginable combinations of smells!

Grandma was waked that night with great dignity, and at dawn when the mourners departed, curiosity overcame an older and more courageous relation than I, to the extent that she insisted we go upstairs and find out if Grandma was wearing a shift beneath her "habit". I agreed reluctantly.

While we peered inside that hideous garment, my companion scarpered, locking the door behind her. To this day, I've never forgotten the stark all-engulfing fear. Strangled screams rose and died in my throat . That horrible man was rising up and coming towards me. I beat my fist on the door until, mercifully, my uncle bounded up the stairs demanding an explanation for the rumpus.

That was my first close encounter with death. The hysteria subsided eventually, but the nightmares lingered on. With time, I began to realise that dead or alive Grandma would never, ever, hurt any of the "childher", despite the fact that we drove her to distraction on countless occasions.

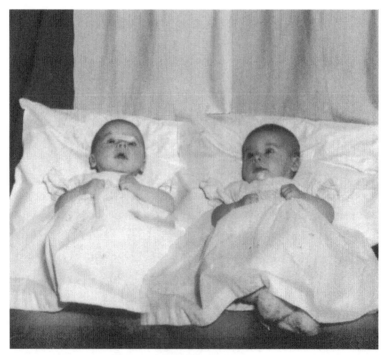

The Twins

18

CHAPTER 3

School: A New Beginning

My first day at school at the age of five did little for my morale. The overcrowded two-roomed building was inhibiting in the extreme. I was a bundle of nerves as I was pushed in the door by another new-comer who had more backbone than I had.

Forty-five pairs of eyes focused with mounting curiosity on my pale scared face and thin bony frame as I was frog-marched towards the teacher's big desk. "The Missus", accustomed as she was to such timidness in first-day fledglings, stepped forward slowly, looking me up and down before saying,

"Now. Who have we here?"

I tried to reply but the words stuck in my throat. Instead, I stammered and stuttered while she became impatient and snapped,

"Speak up girl. We won't bite you".

My eyes fastened on the long yellow cane in her hand as if drawn by a magnet. She must have read my thoughts for she smiled suddenly in what seemed to me in my jittery state to be cold and unfriendly, and continued,

"If you are a good girl you won't get any slaps, but if you are bold......"

The sentence faded away but the inference was clear, as it was in the way she hooped the cane between her hands, releasing it swiftly to let it snap against her silky black dress.

The action spoke volumes, and at that precise moment I would have given anything to be spunky enough to hotfoot it out the door and head for the safety of home.

Satisfied that I had got the message, "The Missus" ushered me to the far end of the room to sit at the infants' desk with all the other five-year olds. We were given crayons, drawing copies and plasticine to do much as we pleased with for the first week. Then the real business commenced, when for the first time in my young life I made feeble attempts to do simple addition in 'TABLE ONE'.

Little did I realise then that I had just sampled the good times in that first week, but fortunately for me and my companions we had no idea that this was the beginning of a long hard grind. Ahead of us was a ten-year stretch of pencil-sucking, errors, cane-walloping.... and let me readily admit .... a generous sprinkling of rebelliousness.

Today I am convinced that this rebellious streak was engendered in us by grown-ups who appeared to be totally lacking in compassion and self-restraint.

Those horrible canes, of which there was an ample supply lurking at the back of the copy-books press, were used on us for the most trivial things, many of which could be resolved with a little bit of patience and understanding. The cruelty of some of these people defied belief. If you were late for school in the morning you started the day with two hard slaps. Minutes later if your sums were wrong you got two more, and so it went all day.

When one of the canes broke during a 'heavy' walloping we almost shrieked with joy, but it was always short-lived. The 'Missus' produced another from the press and hauled her victim across the floor to resume her caning.

One of our female teachers, much younger than the 'Missus', was particularly cross, especially with the five-to-ten year olds who were terrified when she went out of control.

For punishment she had them stand on one leg in the corner of the room, facing the wall for one hour, and woe betide the poor unfortunate who dropped his leg or looked around.

Another of her favourite disciplinary actions was sticking a child's head up the chimney. The child usually resembled a chimney-sweep when permission was granted to withdraw his or her head, and to ensure there would be no more transgression, that youngster was made stand in front of the class while she blistered his legs with the cane.

She pulled handfuls of hair from little girls' heads causing severe pain. Once an enraged parent complained to the parish priest and produced the hair as proof. He was not impressed, and when the parent made a further complaint about the caning her child received he simply said,

"Well, go home now and give her as much more. She shouldn't be carrying stories from school".

Parents were powerless. They came to the school door to see the teacher - threaten her at times, but the child in question always suffered as a result........ with extra beatings for telling at home.

As time progressed the reasons for the "beating-the lessons-into-them" attitude became obvious. The teachers themselves lived in constant fear of being hauled over the coals by the powers–that–be for failing in their duties, and rather than fall foul of authority they tried to force-feed education into us, using the only method that seemed to produce the desired results.

One wonders how they could forget so easily, or ignore the fact that some years previously the lard was beaten out of themselves in the same way.

Did they never cry or fear their teachers as we feared them?

'The Missus' waited after Mass occasionally to walk part of the way home with my mother and update her on her children's performance at school.

She was so kind and charming on those Sunday mornings, touching our cheeks and telling mother what nice little girls we were, "and so bright, Mary".

We went to school on Mondays full of hope that she had changed her opinion of us, but, sadly, she seemed to have forgotten all the nice things she said the previous day. But my mother did not forget, and if one of us dared to carry stories home from school she suspected us of lying. We got a leck in th'ear and were told to get on with our homework.....

We must have deserved it, if we got slapped, she decided.

****

I looked forward to being seven, when I could receive First Holy Communion. That was a major event in our otherwise dreary school lives. Children did not "come to the use of reason" until they were seven years of age and were expected to have full knowledge and understanding of the Sacrament then.

Weeks of preparation went into this momentous occasion. Our noses were stuck in the Penny Catechism until we could recite every line like parrots. Subjects such as Irish and English were put on hold until the great day was over, and the 'Missus' relaxed visibly after the parish priest visited the school and assured himself that each would-be communicant was fully prepared for this solemn celebration.

Saturday was designated as our own special day, away from the prying eyes of the parishioners. Mothers usually arrived with their little ones and handed them over to the 'Missus' who marched each one up to the front seat close to the altar.

As the church ceremony unfolded we sang all our beautiful communion hymns and received the Host for the first time.

The 'Missus' was right behind us, holding our heads to make sure we didn't chew it or spit it out.

After a big build-up it was an equally big let-down to find the Host was virtually tasteless. Some of us expected something sugary. However, it was an improvement on our practice runs for day's beforehand when the 'Missus' cut up newspapers in Host-size pieces, to ensure we all knew how to receive properly on the day. In our eagerness to do the right thing most of us had swallowed the Death Notices in the Irish Press before she could retrieve the paper from our mouths.

The 'Missus' got a new outfit for the day ..... well, almost new. The postmaster managed to discover that she got the loan of it from her sister in Roscommon. A neatly wrapped parcel arrived by post and the postmaster tore a little hole at the edge just to see what was inside. He recognised the colour on the 'Missus' on First Communion Day. One week later a similar parcel was on its way to Roscommon with the same wrapping paper turned inside out. Only the tiniest of tiny holes was required to identify the contents on its return journey.

I didn't feel so bad then about my own outfit. My mother fitted me out in my older sister's communion dress, taking it in here, and letting it out there, with her usual expertise and dainty needlework. Such a beautiful hand-made creation in all its monastic simplicity could, I hoped ..... and it actually did ..... transform my skinny frame and succeeded in bringing a radiant glow of joy to my pale pinched face.

We were all invited to the school afterwards for sweet-cake and biscuits. It was my very first party and nothing could dampen my spirits. Not even the fact that the backside of my beautiful dress became liberally smeared with jam when I accidentally sat on someone's jam roll; nor indeed that the front was generously pock-marked from coming into contact with more sticky fingers than mine. I was dimly aware that there was trouble ahead when I arrived home, but at that moment it mattered not one whit.

"What's another smear?" one might ask off-handedly today, but back in those years there were no stain-removers. Our mothers relied entirely on carbolic soap and the washboard, until Rinso and Lux were introduced to the housewives of Ireland. The former product must have really excelled itself when attempts at restoring the communion dress to its pristine virginal white succeeded.

Father Heaney popped into the school for a few minutes after his breakfast to present each child with a souvenir of their First Holy Communion. This was a sort of mini-scroll with our names and birth-dates inscribed in black and gold paint, and something we were to treasure forever.

Our mothers would be well advised to frame it and send it with those of us who would most assuredly go abroad to earn our living in years to come.

"Today is a great day for all you young people", he declared loudly, rubbing his fingers along his nicotine decorated dentures.

"You are nearer to God today than you ever will be again in your lives".

Before we all went our separate ways he invited us to sing our "May song" once more, *"Bring flowers of the fairest, bring flowers of the rarest............"*, and surprised us by joining in with a resounding,

"Oh Mary, we crown thee with blossoms today,
Queen of the Angels and Queen of the May".

Count John McCormack himself could not have done better.

****

Maytime was always very special.... the month of dedication to the Mother of God. Every home in the country and each classroom in the school produced a statue of the Virgin Mary and surrounded it with flowers in her honour.

Those of us who were deemed trustworthy enough to touch sacred objects inside the altar rails were allowed to assist the adults who adorned Our Lady's Altar in the chapel. Flower-arranging as we know it today was unheard of then, and children were encouraged by their teachers to pick armfuls of wild flowers in the early morning dew, and not just in the fields........ the green banks on the roadside were awash with colour also.

Cowslips, primroses, and bluebells were stuffed into jam-jars or any other receptacles we could find. We squeezed as many as possible into each container and placed them in every available space on the altar. In the midst of the profusion of yellow and white blooms, the Virgin Mary stood serenely beautiful in her long flowing white veil and blue mantle. She inclined her head and smiled benignly down on us.

Over on the far side the Sacred Heart was standing, lonely and forlorn. We felt His sad reproachful eyes watching our every move, and suddenly felt guilty of favouritism. The words of the catechism slowly teased our conscience. "We should love her", it said, "pray to her, pay homage to her, but we should not give her the honour that is due to God alone".

Perhaps it was a bit one-sided to give her all the flowers?

Confusion reigned for a time, but eventually common sense prevailed. June would be His month and He would have the jam-pots and the flowers all to Himself then we reasoned, with obvious relief, careful not to look Him straight in the face as we finished our task and headed out into the brilliant May sunshine.

SOUVENIR OF FIRST COMMUNION

First Communion

CHAPTER 4

School Holidays

The hands of the clock moved with infuriating lack of speed before I reached the age of nine. Summer holidays were well under way, and I could easily be forgiven for wondering if they ever heard the word 'holiday' in our house. Work went on as usual.... the small tasks delegated to my siblings and I seemed to pile up like a snowdrift. Washing the clay off buckets of potatoes with the handle of the twig to fill the pigs pot for boiling; carrying water from the village well in small tin-cans made by a well-known family of tinsmiths, who resided by the waterfall through the summer months; feeding the hens and collecting the eggs, and woe betide anyone who dropped even one egg. Bringing in turf for the fire was ongoing. The turf-box in the corner of the kitchen seemed to be empty almost as soon as we filled it. The list of small tasks was endless.

We were not to know that all those jobs were an exercise in restriction of movement for the sole purpose of preventing us from gadding about the village all day. Most times we came back with our clothes well torn from traipsing through the bushes in search of blackberries or sloes... even haws if we could find nothing else. A spate of mending usually followed for our much annoyed mother who kept repeating,

"Have ye anything at all to do besides tearin' ye'r clothes?"

Perhaps it was not so surprising after all, that she well and truly kept our noses to the grindstone, rather than spending time patching and mending our shredded threadbare garments.

My father rarely noticed our absence unless he needed our assistance outside, and then he shouted furiously,

"Are them gone gallivantin' again, or fot?"

We returned quickly if we were within hearing distance when my mother called out to us, knowing what lay in store if we ignored her.

Tempers ran high occasionally. Our dissenting voices could be heard from time to time. We assumed we were the only children who had 'jobs' to do and we rebelled with delaying tactics when we were sent off to the well for at least the tenth time. That proved to be a foolish move on our part. We paid the price later.

Ah, Grandma, Grandma, wherever you are today, you and your ilk were not the only ones who believed in the power of the rod. You left a good legacy behind. We have discovered that your descendants can apply generous measures of that same treatment whenever we try to outsmart them, we acknowledged silently.

Memories abide of the tripod, known to all as the trippet, hanging on the wall beside the fireplace in our kitchen, and reclining on that trippet for all to see was that god-awful rod. When neighbours or relations came for a visit they joked about the item that held pride of place in our house, and we wondered, not for the first time, how adults could laugh and be so insensitive about that dreaded rod.

From where I'm sitting now, I must admit, however reluctantly, that rod was the only language we understood. Without it the nation's parents would never instill any obedience in their offspring, and for our gang it certainly was a great deterrent when temptation beckoned. One glance in its direction, perched on the trippet, ever-ready to oblige, warned even the most courageous of us to backtrack.

On occasion when my mothers patience was sorely tried and she threatened to "warm our backsides", we entered into negotiations with her, appealing for clemency and promising to do all sorts of tasks.... forever if need be... anything at all to sweet-talk her into dropping the charges against us. This particular barter rarely worked. The half-finished tasks spilled over to the next day when we assumed all would be forgotten. But my mother's crystal clear memory was more than we bargained for.

****

Cutting and saving the hay was exciting for a few days and then, like everything else, it became another weary chore. Every day my father cut a little bit more with his scythe, and every day we had to work a little bit harder to turn and re-turn the long lines of hay withering away in the heat of the sun. To this day I am amazed that he trusted under-nines with hayforks. We could have sunk them into our bare feet, but he believed, as all the men of his day did, that if we got a "little sthob" we would make absolutely sure it didn't happen again.

After three days of scorching hot weather the hay was made into small cocks to safeguard it from the rain that MIGHT fall in the night, and finally it was fit for tramping into big cocks. These would be transferred to the haggard later on, and the lot put into one huge pile called a sheep-cock with a pole in the centre. A fair bit of eye-balling went into trimming, shaping and raking down this giant hay-stack. My father walked around it umpteen times before he pronounced himself satisfied with the end result.

"Tis fit for trampin' today, Michael", the neighbours remarked on the way to their own meadows to perform a similar task.

"I s'pose" was the cool reply.

My father had a great economy with words when he was depending on the clouds for the weather forecast, and someone leaning over the wall for a leisurely chat was the last thing he wanted while his entire workforce stood by impatiently awaiting his instructions.

The customary row ensued as to which one of us would be selected to tramp the hay. If the mood was good, two were hoisted up to commence tramping and three more stood sulking on the ground despite being aware that their turn would come before the day ended.

It was all very pleasant for a few hours, but we were heartily sick of the hard slog by the time the Neale chapel bell was ringing out the Angelus at six o'clock. We were still at it when the sun began to dip down behind Maamturk mountains, and a chill had crept into the field. Tears of frustration were close. We wanted to go home, but my father insisted on getting all the hay "up", because "tomorrow could be a down-wet day".

He knew his stuff when it came to getting the most out of youngsters - willing or otherwise. He believed that bending down could not possibly present any problems for us, and could not accept that at the end of a long day our young backs ached almost as much as his did. Worse still, our feet had numerous thistle-thorns embedded in them from walking barefoot all day. We limped home, either on our toes or our heels, depending on the part of the foot that hurt most. My mother performed surgery for an hour, prodding our tender flesh with a fine sewing needle to locate and remove the offending thorns, and finally a dab of Jeyes Fluid on what closely resembled minced steak completed the operation... until the morrow when she held her clinic all over again. This was a painful procedure, but slightly more bearable than the punishing jabs inflicted with every step we took.

We whimpered at first contact with the needle, and even cried a little, jerking our feet from mothers grasp and sending the needle flying across the kitchen floor.

30

"Ye'll get a leck in th'ear if ye'r not careful", my father threatened with little sympathy.

Well! He should talk. He had shoes and socks on all day. We wiped our tears in silent resentment, and passionately wished we could stick that awful needle into his lean backside as he walked out the door.

****

Now that the hay was "up", my father reluctantly cycled ten miles to the bog to spend a day "turnin' out" turf, wheeling it out to the sand road in a wheelbarrow in preparation for loading it into the horse-cart the following day. He worked late into the evening and arrived home, as he usually did, just as dusk was descending on the village.

That same evening my mother shooed all of us outside, and locked the door while she went to the village well for two buckets of water. She couldn't leave us indoors as there was always the possibility that one or two of us would "start fiddlin'" with the open fire in her absence.

I was left in charge with strict instructions not to let the younger ones out of my sight.

"Not even for one second or you'll get a leck in th'ear when I come back", she warned, but, alas all of this was wasted on her unheeding offspring. She hadn't got her heels past the cart-house before I was standing up on the long stone seat at the front door, demanding attention from the others. I was going to sing and they would be allowed to join in. I was on stage with a captive audience, enthralled with the sound of my own voice in the eerie silence of the deepening dusk. I neither knew nor cared what was happening around me.

My mother returned in twenty minutes to find the third youngest missing, and despite all our efforts we failed to find him. There was absolute mayhem and fears for his safety as the minutes turned into an hour. He must surely be sucked into a "swally-hole" in the 'Léna' by now! Or perhaps he was eaten alive by one of those awful savage beasts that hadn't yet invaded our part of the world! He would never return and it was all my fault.

We searched frantically in the hen-house, the duck-house, the stable, and the fields. We called his name, but our echo kept coming back to us. We inquired discreetly in the village houses without giving anything away.

"Mammy wants to put him to bed", we lied, knowing she didn't wish to go public and look a right fool if he was just hiding all the time.

She was demented. Her beloved "Danno" was gone forever. He was a solid "butt" of a young lad - three years old - and well able to use his fists. He was nick-named "Danno" by a neighbour, after the celebrated boxer of the day... Dan O'Mahoney. Mother could only pray that he would now be as tough as the real Danno, who featured so prominently in the Irish Press a week earlier.

In the midst of the hullabaloo, when I was about to receive yet another stinging wallop across the face for my negligence, my father arrived on the scene carrying Danno on the bar of the bike. Apparently he had wandered to an isolated area of the village and kept going ahead, alone and frightened. Fortunately, he was picked up by a farmer doing a late-evening count on his sheep, who had a good idea of the parentage, and was about to return him to the fold when my father came by on his bicycle.

Danno was none the worse for his experience, but I got yet another sharp leck in th'ear for lettin' 'im go.

Neither parent could understand that I was so full up of my own importance I failed to notice a shortfall in the numbers around me.

The punishment was severe. I was ordered to draw enough water from the well to fill the barrels at the back of the house. It was so unfair, I protested bitterly. After all, Paddy broke three eggs when he stuck his hand under the clockin' hen a week earlier, and he got away scot-free.

It was a dreadful evening for all of us, and for me in particular. I was sunk in misery, tears of self-pity flowing copiously. It was made abundantly clear that I would never be left in charge again, and my singing debut which opened on such a high note, now lay in ruins around me.

Sleep was impossible that night. I crept out of bed very early before the dawn broke. It was then I noticed that the darkest time of the night was just before the dawn. When the light came, it came very gradually, and very gently, and pulled the mantle of darkness away from the world, and there was a new day. It was a profoundly moving and unforgettable experience, for a young tearaway such as I was, and that particular new day was never more welcome..........

A Day in the Bog

33

CHAPTER 5

The Concert

Despite the working holidays and all the whinging, we were decidedly reluctant to present ourselves in Cross school in September. If truth were told, this applied not just to us but to every single child in every national school throughout the country.

We were a dismal-looking lot, all seven of us, like steps of stairs, running down "th'oul road", terrified of being late and earning two hard slaps of the cane on our first day back at school. We could see the Whelans and the Hughes ahead of us, but we failed to narrow the distance between us. They were also running like hares, and just managed to scramble into the old familiar seats before roll-call.

We had advance warning that we would have a new teacher after the holidays, so perhaps it was reasonable that we should be rather apprehensive on her first day. We expected to meet another unbending, unfriendly female, but were pleasantly surprised to find that our new Miss Duffy was young and smiling and eager to be acquainted with us. We couldn't tear our eyes away from her clothes, or her hair, or her shoes. Here was a "Modern Miss" wearing a gorgeous grey check costume with a red silk blouse, and the lapels of the jacket trimmed with a matching red. It was a delightful change, far removed from the depressing black dress worn by the 'Missus' since we first started school. Two days went by before any of us noticed that the black dress had a slightly different look. The plunging V neckline was discreetly camouflaged by inserting a dainty piece of lace inside the lower end of the V, giving it a softer feminine look. It was also very effectual in concealing her "things" from our inquisitive young eyes each time she leaned forward to correct our copy-books.

Suddenly, a whole new world opened up for us. Within two weeks the cold bare walls of the classroom were awash with colour. Miss Duffy was a genius. She painted pictures of farmers ploughing in the spring-time, with seagulls flying overhead watching out for worms. She painted women milking cows; frisky young lambs; cats, dogs, pigs, hens - and they all looked so clean and cuddly, unlike the ones in our fields at home.

She made beautiful pictures of little boys and girls climbing gates, skipping, playing ball, tumbling, and all of them with happy laughing faces. We feasted our eyes on them and heard not one word when morning prayers were recited by the 'Missus'.

We were full of inspiration. Coloured chalks began to disappear from the school press, and we coloured in anything we could lay our hands on when we got home in the evenings. Even our barn door got the works. Well-endowed young beauties suddenly emerged from our endeavours, and seemed to smile coquettishly at the middle-aged village men. I myself coloured what I considered to be a masterpiece. I hadn't been looking down the 'Missus'' V neck for nothing, and I hoped and prayed that the rain would never fall again to wash it off.

Not so with my father. He was certainly not artistic, and he was also hopping mad. I was ordered to go and blot that off the door quick, and stop actin' like a bloody *amadhaun*. I was totally crushed by what I presumed to be such undeserving anger, and nursed my grievances privately for three or four evenings afterwards, lying on the sheet-iron roof of the pig-house - away from my fathers angry scowl. He rarely came near the place. That was my mother's domain, and I made sure I climbed down before her rescue team organized a search party. The Danno incident remained in my mind, and at nine-and-a-half I could not expect to get off lightly.

If anyone but myself was describing me they would probably say I was a rebellious little urchin, and they would probably be right. But the severity of the "sentences", and the frustration that followed left a lot to be desired. There was great comfort to be gained from the knowledge that everyone's children got the same tough treatment. It was not that they didn't love us. They did. But they felt duty-bound at all times to raise us as good, honest, God-fearing Christians, in the same way they themselves were raised.

****

All of this faded into the background of my memory very quickly when Miss Duffy hinted at some thrilling event about to take place in the school. The parish priest decided to organize a children's variety concert in a fund-raising effort to reconstruct the rapidly deteriorating schoolrooms. After long and varied discussions with the teachers, the enormous task of bringing the concert to fruition was placed in Miss Duffy's hands, much to the surprise of the 'Missus'. But fortunately for all concerned - and the school - she proved herself both capable and talented, guiding the 'players' to the opening night like a true professional.

Many weeks of training and preparation went into this delightful undertaking. For me, the whole world changed. School was no longer a nightmare. We sang and we danced, and once again, as for First Holy Communion, all the usual subjects were put on hold until the concert was over. I was not alone in wishing it would go on like this for evermore.

Imagine my surprise when I - of all people - was chosen to play the leading part as *"Banraoighn na Sídheóg"* (Queen of the Fairies) in a two-act Irish play entitled *"Tír-na-nÓg"*. A neighbour's boy was selected to play the *"Greasaí*

Leprecháun" beside me, and despite a diffident beginning we established a reasonably good rapport in our very important roles.

The communion dress of two years ago was destined to make another public appearance, and at Miss Duffy's request my mother was hastily undoing the seams once again to accommodate my slowly developing body. This favour was requested on a Sunday, and it was a blessed relief to find there was no sewing involved. Grandma always said "Anything you sew on Sundays must be ripped with your nose on the Last Day".

"An' I have no intention", my mother snapped, "of kneeling before St. Peter, rippin' that communion dress in front of the whole village".

Our teacher-cum-director took over from my mother and converted the dress into a gown fit for a queen. She began by stitching on a multi-panelled, star-spangled long satin skirt, adorned at the back with a huge frothy bow. My crown she deftly fashioned from one of the strong brown, four-pound, sugar-bags of the day, then painted it with "Gold Leaf" used for painting picture frames. The stones from a broken "glass" rosary beads were recycled as diamonds, which were glued on when the "Gold Leaf" dried out.

To complete the picture, she cut one of those dreaded yellow canes down to the required size, reached for the sugar-bags once again, to cut out and paint a gold star which she glued to one end of the cane, and joy of joys!, suddenly I was waving my magic wand.

I brandished it about imperiously, half convinced that I was indeed a real queen. I cast my magic spell on the little "woodland fairies" who immediately fell into a deep slumber at a single wave of my charmed baton.

That was my first and only taste of real power. I floated on stage majestically on the big night, aware that none would dare to disobey the Queen of the Fairies. Or so I thought, until one of the woodland elves hissed close beside me,

"Ya think ya're great, Éaneen Shaughnessy. We'll getcha in the playground tomorrow".

Suddenly I felt my great surge of power abating, but then, as my beautiful gown winked and sparkled encouragingly in the lights from the four paraffin oil lamps hanging well above our heads, I was swept along on a tide of restored jubilation.

I played my part well, as did all the cast. We remembered every line, gesture and movement and got a standing ovation when the final curtain came down.

Miss Duffy heard the earlier on-stage threat and warned that we would immediately be replaced by our stand-ins if we dared to misbehave, and frightened of demotion, we pretended an off-stage friendship, but I knew by the look in her eye that my adversary would resume hostilities when the performance ended on the second night. I was not disappointed.

The concert was well supported by parents and friends, who took turns to attend both shows and gaze in admiration at their off-spring in action - each parent privately convinced that their own little babes were the stars of the show. It took strength of character to actually come and pay to see something they must have been heartily sick of for weeks beforehand. My own mother, for one, was already familiar with every song and dance routine in the variety show preceding "*Tír-na-nÓg*".

Throughout the first night the "*Greasaí Leprecháun's*" mother looked anxious and ill at ease. That little man with the green jacket and the long white beard, who was obliged to mend shoes for the duration of the show, was taking his role much too seriously. A hammer and a 'last' were provided for the repairs, with explicit instructions not to hit too hard, and his mother watched in angry silence as her little horror hammered the hell out of the only good pair of shoes he possessed.

Well, she'd teach him. A sharp stinging from a bunch of nettles - her favourite punishment - should curb his heavy-handedness with the hammer, she thought wrathfully. Fortunately for the *Leprechaun*, no serious damage was done, but it certainly wasn't for want of trying.

Overall, the concert was a great success. The priest purred with satisfaction and plans were put in place immediately to give our school its much needed face-lift. Work was to be carried out during the school vacation period, but in his eagerness to embark on the project, the P.P. had workmen on the site three weeks beforehand, and the entire school population was re-located in the chapel, until the official school closing date. Teachers were at their wits end. There was no water, no toilets, and no privacy other than to seek refuge behind the old yew trees when nature called. The smell was unbearable and adults were forced to tread carefully on their way to Sunday Mass. Some of us wet ourselves daily and had angry-looking raw sores on our bottoms which we were too embarrassed to mention at home. Instead, we dusted ourselves liberally with Robin Starch, which was the equivalent of baby-powder at the time. More trouble was in store when we failed to account for the near empty carton, which was kept solely for the youngest baby in the house.

To speed up the work and reduce costs, a voluntary labour rota was set up in the parish, sometimes to the secret annoyance of farmers who had hay "down" when it was their turn to give a couple of days, but they could not risk the priest's wrath by refusing to co-operate. However, it all seemed worthwhile when a fine building began to emerge from all the rubble......

We scarcely recognised the place when the school re-opened. Gone were all the old broken forms, and shiny new two-seater desks stood proudly in their place. The dark brown wainscotting on the lower part of the schoolroom walls had been torn down, and not surprisingly, vast numbers of a prolific rat family were homeless as a result.

We had become experts on smells... rats, drains, dry-rot and damp. Rats droppings were a familiar sight on the floor in the mornings. The 'Missus' assured herself that this resulted from careless pupils leaving doors open in the evenings.

Obviously, she did not realise the rats had taken up residence behind the timber long before her time.

The damp and dismal building, clocking up almost a century, was gone forever. Three new rooms welcomed us, looking splendid in the obligatory green and cream paint. If only the 'Missus' wasn't standing there in her dreary depressing black dress spoiling it all.....

We didn't have to wait very long to see the last of her. She did not enjoy the new school for any length of time. Shortly after re-opening she became too ill to teach, and eventually a "sub" was appointed to replace her. We never saw her again and, sadly, we neither knew nor cared what happened to her.

Singing the Night Away

CHAPTER 6

Father Heaney P.P.

"A taste o' the grass makes a rogue o' the cow". She's sure to come back for more. So it was with Father Heaney. Such phenomenal success with the concert fired his enthusiasm to the extent that he saw it as a means of resolving a considerable portion of the parish financial problems.

Two more concerts followed. Local tradesmen worked long hours at night to erect the stage once again in the master's room. The most consistent worker of all was an industrial school boy, now a grown young man of twenty, who worked for a local farmer for four years. He had a distinctive flair for organizing and gave freely of his time and talent.

He supported Miss Duffy right through to the final curtain, having enormous respect for a lady who treated him as an equal and relied on his invaluable contribution to the success of the night.

He had his own solo spot in the variety show and sang *"She moved through the fair"* with a panache that even John McNally would be proud of today.

A far cry, one might say, from the strict regime of Letterfrack and all the other industrial schools in the country, where the inmates were seldom seen and rarely ever heard.

Weeks later, when weather permitted, we had an *Aeríocht* - or Field Day as it is known today, in a field close to Cross school.

My sister walked away with medals for each of her performances... a reel, a jig, a hornpipe and two Irish songs.

No one was surprised. She had a natural talent for both singing and dancing.

The day ended with a seven-aside football match, an event which attracted young men from outlying parishes and contributed substantially to the takings for the day. Fr. Heaney had enough in the kitty to purchase the harmonium so urgently needed by Miss Duffy. She would no longer be beholden to Cong school for the loan of their piano each time she produced a concert, and he already discussed plans for putting together a chapel choir, selected and trained by her alone.

He needed five new sets of vestments in their various shades of black, white, purple, green and red. These were costly items despite the fact that nuns did all the embroidery on such precious and sacred robes. Money was scarce, and parishioners were slow to co-operate.....

The Mass Missal was in tatters, but fortunately for the P.P. a new one was very generously donated by an old lady from our own village whom we called Grandmother. It cost all of £9 at the time, and everyone marvelled at the wealth of the woman who looked as if she didn't have tuppence to her name. She firmly believed she was doing it for God, and what better way to get a "leg in" with her Lord and Master, now that she was ninety and due to meet Him face to face soon.

"Strike while the iron is hot", was the P.P's motto. He was lavish in his praise for the old lady and sternly rebuked those who were lax in their duties. Proposing to name names invariably produced good results, but pressure had to be maintained, otherwise, some of his flock quickly reverted to paying the old contribution of a few pennies at the chapel door.

Grievous mortal sin was committed by overrating worldly goods, he reminded his hard-up listeners. Now was the time to dig into the old feather mattresses and share their wealth with God.

A quote from the Bible proved very effective; "What doth it profit a man if he gain the whole world and suffer the loss of his immortal soul".

Equally effective was another quote, delivered in impassioned tones, "It is easier for a camel to pass through the eye of a needle, than for a rich man to enter the Kingdom of Heaven".

Throughout the summer when Yanks were home from America, the P. P. always managed to meet them and greet them, and update them on his latest parish projects. Loud praise ensued for his exemplary efforts. Shiny handbags were opened up and several dollars found their way into the overjoyed P.Ps back pocket. With such generosity he could purchase all his requirements for his beloved chapel very soon.

One of those Yanks was my father's cousin, and I still remember her rather strange request when she visited our house. She asked for one sod of turf; a few cabbage leaves; a wedge of home-cured salty bacon and a potato... to take back to Boston. Later in her Christmas letter, all was revealed. She boiled the bacon, cabbage, and potato for dinner; sat at the table with the sod of turf under her feet, and bragged to her family that she was eating an Irish dinner on Irish soil!

Accepting change is never easy particularly when it involves money. Parishioners now had a choice of having High Mass or Low Mass offered up for their relatives at the time of their death. Hitherto, they knew of none other than the time-honoured Low Mass for both funerals and the Sabbath Day, and for which they had a deep reverence and appreciation, but they were more than sceptical about this new-fangled High Mass thrust upon them at a time when an enforced increase in contributions was such a sore point.

43

"High Mass for high money, Low Mass for low money, and No Mass for no money". So said the irate church-goers when the P.P. introduced the new Mass, which would cost a whopping £1.

Nothing would be a secret henceforth, the faithful exclaimed heatedly, on reflection. A family's financial status would now be determined by their choice of Mass for their loved ones, as the P.P. was well aware. Predictably, Low Mass for funerals became virtually non-existent in the coming months. Few could afford the £1, but beg or borrow, they honoured their obligations when paradise beckoned.

Only the best was good enough, the bereaved declared stoutly, although there were occasions when some privately thought the late-lamented were undeserving of such an expensive farewell, but illusions of affluence had to be maintained throughout those difficult days.

Concelebrated Mass, as it became known, was solemnized by five priests singing the Mass, rather than reading from the missal in the traditional manner, and the responses were sung by the newly-formed adult choir conducted by Miss Duffy. The priests sat on chairs with their backs to the congregation, their outer vestment, known as 'The Chasuble', draped over the altar rails behind them. Their singing was deplorable, and cheeky amateurs we might be, but we certainly recognised non-singers when we heard them.

"Réquiem aetérnaum, dó-na éis, Dóminé", they chanted in low mournful tones, while women wept silently, but heartless rascals that we were, we giggled helplessly throughout the Mass, causing our teacher to reconsider the wisdom of allowing us to skip class with a view to educating us on the new ceremony.

Women were expected to wear a complete black outfit for an official mourning period of one year following a family bereavement. White handkerchiefs with black edging complemented this ensemble, but those who were unable to afford such luxuries resigned themselves to wearing a black armband or a black "diamond" stitched to their coat sleeve. The manufacturers of "Drummer Dyes" did well. If a jacket or coat could "take" black dye, many problems were solved without financial strain.

In those same years the upper classes considered it disrespectful to correspond with their friends without mourning stationery - white notepaper and envelopes - both deeply edged with black.

One of the least acceptable traditions during the mourning period was the cessation of all social activities outside the home. Young girls were denied the pleasure of going dancing on Sunday nights. Singing was prohibited, as was courting. Many a girl tried in vain to keep her romance alive by meeting her village beau "accidentally" when she ran to the well at sundown for a bucket of water, and he was on his way to Cross for five Woodbines and a chat with the lads.

The restrictive practices imposed on young women did not apply so rigidly to the young men, most of whom silently rebelled against such antiquated customs, and sneaked out to the local dances without parental approval. Fathers suddenly found themselves being "fair-minded" and unable to pursue the family arguments which followed the discovery of these moonlight flits. They cherished their own freedom of movement greatly, and while they might not go dancing like their sons, they certainly found solace in the village pubs where they enjoyed a good pint and the occasional sing-song.

Mothers, realising they were standing alone on this thorny issue, eventually bowed to the inevitable, and from there on the onus lay more or less in the female domain.

The P.P. flared up. Those boyos were up to no good, he predicted. He knew only too well what all young scamps anticipated when they gathered together at the local hop. It was time to instill some real fear into them. Every Sunday he thundered on about sins of the flesh, impure thoughts, temptation and lust. All of which had to be confessed before they attempted to go near the altar for communion.

Their greatest anxiety was his constant threat to "turf mortal sinners out of his confessional", and leave them with no choice other than go to the Bishop for absolution.

Finding ways and means of getting to Tuam, where the Bishop resided, would pose problems for most people in those days. There was but one hackney car in the locality and the driver was not renowned for his discretion. Numerous questions would arise, and none would admit having to go before His Lordship.

It rarely, if ever, happened. Young men solved their dilemma in their own way, when occasionally they were requested to leave the confessional without absolution. Confessions were heard in Ballinrobe chapel on Saturday nights from seven to nine o'clock, and under the pretext of going for a hair-cut, young lads cycled five miles into town, arriving at the chapel when the priest was unable to stifle his yawns, and longing to retire to the comfort of his sitting room where a blazing turf fire awaited him.

It would be a "rush job", they knew from experience, and their confessor's lack of interest encouraged them to skip the mortal sins allegedly committed the previous week, and deal with venial ones only. This was hastily followed by an important prayer, taught in their school days, especially for genuine omission of sins, or for the contrite offender who wished to seek forgiveness more than once for past transgressions.

"For these, and all the sins of my past life, O Lord forgive me", they prayed devoutly.

The priest absolved them readily, and the lads attended Sodality next morning with "souls as pure as the driven snow".

Perhaps the most thankless, self-imposed duty for the priest was patrolling the roads in the vicinity of Cong dance-hall after midnight on Sunday nights, with the intention of separating courting couples.

I remember my father telling a neighbour "the priest foll-ied the lads last night, an' he gave them hell, an' called them tom-cats on the prowl". Both roared with laughter at the thought.

The fact that the dance-hall was privately owned did not deter his Reverence from popping inside occasionally to assure himself that males and females did not mingle, but innocent man that he was in affairs of the heart, he was unable to read the body language, and the lads managed to date their partners during the last dance of the night, right under his clerical eye. They scattered in all directions, leaping over walls, into the fields, when he caught them unawares later.

A wily young rascal feigned a broken ankle once, when the P.P. found him on the roadside. "Get help, Father", he rasped in agony, hoping to move him on quickly. He was, in fact, awaiting the return of the P.P's own housemaid who scarpered into the bushes as the priest strode towards them, and having bragged earlier that he wooed her with "a quarther o' bulls eyes", he was not going home till he got his moneys worth.

One quick-witted character, strolling along with his mature lady-friend on one such night was heard to remark jovially after the chase,

"The P.P. did ME a great favour, anyway. Only for HIM, I'd never have got her inside the wall"

47

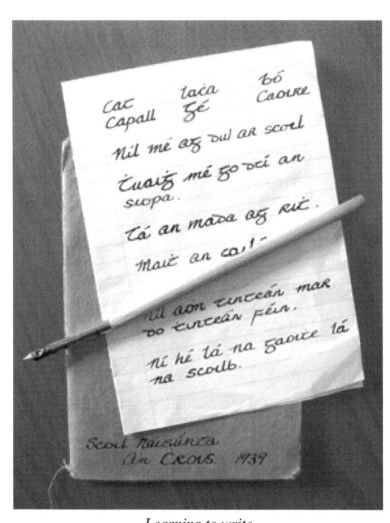

Learning to write

CHAPTER 7

The Village

Perhaps the most notable aspect of the village of Houndswood where I was born and reared was its apparently insurmountable hills and deep sloping hollows. A cyclist pedalling at a reasonable speed on the long stretch of sand road through Houndswood to the Waterfall could only be compared to a canoeist in his little boat, bobbing up and down between turbulent waves on a stormy ocean.

"Th'oul 'road", as it is still known, was once the main line to Galway, but in later years a new road, predictably named "The New Line", was constructed, and while it might not have the hills and hollows it certainly had its fair share of long winding stretches and dangerous corners.

The Houndswood hills oft times tested the patience of the village people, especially on Sunday mornings when all were rushing for nine-thirty Mass - the only one of the day, or indeed the week.

Beating the clock and climbing the long hills left them panting and red-faced, particularly the men, following a hectic morning "doin' th'outside jobs". The obligatory farm chores would be completed for the day, whenever possible, before they got cleaned up for Mass. Sunday was their official off-duty day, leaving them with time for a good snooze or a chat with the neighbours.

"Remember thou keep holy the Sabbath Day" was resolutely adhered to in the male domain, but little thought was spared for the women who had to wash and dress six or seven children before they could think of "throwin' a dhrop o'wather" on their own faces, when they also started beating the clock and climbing the hills with all their little chicks in tow. After Mass, they hurried home, changed into their week-day clothes and got on with the cooking and housework as usual.

However, if there was a bad summer and saving the hay proved difficult, the men hoped the Lord would forgive them, silently promising to mention it in confessions the next Sodality Saturday, and went out with a fork to give a turn to the hay, still wearing the good Sunday suit and tie.

How incongruous it would look today to see a man dressed up in his best bib- and- tucker driving a David Brown tractor in a twenty-acre field of hay!

Country homes had no running water and no bathrooms in my youth, and Houndswood was no exception. The smell of strong tobacco and sweat lingered around most men, until Sunday morning, when they shaved with carbolic soap. The great romantics of the nineties would have us believe their unwashed state was the "raw masculine scent of him". One wonders how the more offensive farm smells of today would be defined. Not as a stimulus, surely, as anyone who has been close to a farmer feeding silage to his cattle, or agitating his slurry-pit can verify.

For our own water supply we relied mainly on three good spring wells in the village. The barrel at the back of our house holding the spill from the thatch was used for washdays, and while our parents prayed for fine weather, we certainly prayed for rain. Our arms ached from drawing buckets of water to fill the barrel for washday during a dry spell, and it was not entirely unknown for the cow to steal a march and reduce the contents of that same barrel to half within seconds. We had no option other than hurry home from school and start all over again next day.

Close to home was a great well in Tobernineen, the local graveyard, reputedly the best water in the locality for its teeth-chattering coldness, even in mid-summer. Many people believed it wasn't right to drink the water as the well was located in the graveyard, but hastily changed their minds when the other watering-holes ran low. However, sixty years on, it is still used and still acclaimed to be of excellent quality despite any doubts some might harbour.

This ancient burial ground dates back to the eighteenth century and was chosen mostly for babies who were still-born, or who lived but a few hours or perhaps a day. It was not unusual in my time to go to the well in the morning and see a freshly dug grave close by the stone wall. Substantial evidence that a father or perhaps a friend arrived with the swirling grey mists of dawn and silently laid a little babe to rest, then just as silently crept away again before the neighbourhood woke up. Despite the secrecy, the neighbours could always guess the identity of the recently interred infant, but it was never referred to in the presence of the family concerned.

At school, we learned from our curate, Fr. Lyons, that Tobernineen should be pronounced Tober-i-neen, meaning Ina's Well, and that once upon a time there actually was a Saint Ina. So enamoured were we with such a beautiful name, we succeeded in persuading our parents into bestowing it upon the latest and last member of our large family. I suspect my mother hoped to witness the resurrection of another such saint, or perhaps a nun, but alas, all hope vanished as her angelic little cherub slowly but surely began to emerge as a distinctly acrobatic tom-boy. Visions of sainthood were consigned to the dim recesses of mother's mind forever.

Although this tranquil little graveyard is mainly a plot for children, among them one of our own family, there are some adults sleeping there also, including the family on whose property this sacred ground is situated. This small green corner beneath God's clear blue skies, almost invisible except to those who know its whereabouts, is still one of Ireland's most peaceful resting places.

Further south in the village are the ruins of Houndswood House, a splendid 18th century dwelling once owned by John S. Dawson. In my youth the tumble-down residence was generally known as Grants - presumably purchased in later years by someone bearing that name. Land-holder Dawson was the owner of approximately eleven hundred and thirty acres in Houndswood, of which about two hundred and fifteen acres were leased to thirty-seven tenants, among them my own ancestors, the Shaughnessys. The descendants of many of these tenants still occupy that same land, and one of the cottages in which they resided is still standing.

For some inexplicable reason the village of Houndswood was often referred to as "Tón-Rúadh". A mere trifling to my way of thinking but one which irritated some people occasionally. Translated, the name simply meant "Red arse", "red backside", "red bottom", take your pick - and not even Mrs Mahoney from Cross with her brilliant razor-sharp memory, and parish folklore at her finger-tips could identify its origin.

Rumours abounded that Houndswood House, or Grants as we knew it, was haunted and anyone who dared to trespass risked life and limb. There was a huge orchard to the rear of the former main residence, surrounded by stone-built high walls on all sides, and as one approached the locked heavy-duty gates the feeling of being watched was scary, even in daylight, almost as if a silent sentinel stood behind the overgrown neglected shrubs, waiting and ready to pounce.

Equally alarming was the local perception that while some people actually gained entry to steal a bag of apples, not one could say they ever sampled one apple. Immediately they dropped down inside the high walls, gale-force winds, whipping into a hurricane, swept across the garden. Trees were uprooted; branches torn asunder; and apples pelted in all directions. The raiders retreated in fear and trembling, glad to escape from the wicked phantom within.

The more brazen members of our family, myself included, decided to ignore the ghost stories, climbing - just once - over the walls with a great exhibition of bravado that was far from genuine, considering the mass of goose-pimples appearing all over our flesh.

Our teeth were chattering as we picked our way through nettles and briars. Just then a younger member of the clan insisted there was a horrible man, like an elephant, behind the trees watching us. Sheer terror took over, restricting our efforts to reach the walls. In an instant the much-publicised hurricane was sweeping towards us. Apples were hurled in our direction, and millions of leaves went scurrying past us like a multitude of angry wasps. We tripped and fell in our mad scramble to reach the safety of the outside world. We screamed aloud but no sounds came, and totally hysterical, we finally vaulted over the wall like greyhounds, badly shaken and bruised.

We threw ourselves on the ground, unable to move for several long moments. Eventually we regained our composure and peered through a small hole in the wall, but all was unnervingly calm inside with not a trace of the turbulence we felt sure we had just witnessed. The trees were snoozing comfortably under the weight of tons of apples in the warm September sunshine, while the lush green leaves looked like they had a firm hold on life for at least another month.

We were the stalwart youths who had intended to hide behind the bushes to get a glimpse of the big man in the long black trench-coat and the black hard hat, reputedly seen on numerous occasions riding his milk-white steed down to the spring well situated outside the boundary wall. Having drunk from the cool clear spring, rider and horse retraced their steps and then vanished. For all we cared they could both drown.

We had enough. We tore home to report our hair-raising experience but my father quickly deflated our exuberance, muttering,

"Good enough fo'ye. Fot brought ye innit? The like o'ye should have enough o'sense..."

Did he mean enough sense not to go there, or enough sense not to believe in ghost stories? We never found out.

****

Houndswood had more than its fair share of raggle-taggle tinkers camping each year in an area known to all as the Waterfall. The words 'itinerant', 'new age traveller', or 'knight of the road' were unheard of in those days. These people were known simply as 'the tinkers' and they accepted that with calm indifference.

They pulled into the village with a random assortment of piebald ponies, asses, foals, dogs and goats. Trailing in the wake of this spectacle were two or three carts bearing women and children, while the men, recently revitalized with a few "half-ones", trudged alongside smoking Woodbines.

Some arrived quietly at sundown, while others made a noisy entrance to the village after closing-time in the pubs. They had the good and the bad among them, but in fairness, the good ones far outweighed the bad ones, and in fairness also, they were well treated by the village people who firmly believed "If you only give a cup o'wather in God's name, you will be rewarded in Heaven".

The women and children begged from door to door all day. Milk, flour, eggs or potatoes were usually given when they asked "Would'ya have a charity Ma'am, an' God blesh'a?"

Occasionally they refused potatoes, claiming they were already overloaded, but gratefully accepted tea or sugar instead. Most of those women were nursing mothers with a baby tucked under their shawl, presumably feeding, leaving the mother looking drained and tired. My own mother had a certain empathy with them, giving a little extra whenever possible until my father, always sceptical, discovered one day that the new baby was not always quite as "new" as they would have people believe.

"A young lad hopped out from under 'er gansey an' legged it down the road the minnit she went out that door", he exclaimed wrathfully.

"That crowd think we're eejits", he added furiously, harking back to the damage done the previous week when the blackguards among them let their horses loose on an unsuspecting village at midnight, destroying crops of wheat and oats. While the locals were raging, nothing was actually said to the culprits, but they could sense a withdrawal of charities and sympathy, particularly in the houses where the women always treated them with consideration, and they wondered in a bemused sort of way, "Fot did we do on them?"

They were their own worst enemies.

It was common knowledge that they put an 'X' mark on the wall close to the houses where they were well received. If so, they must have at least two 'Xs' outside every home in Houndswood, but however hard we tried, we never, ever found them.

Th'oul Road: Houndswood

CHAPTER 8

Travellin' On

"We should be educated enough so we don't have to look up to anyone, but wise enough not to look down on anyone".

Such wisdom would not have gone amiss among the travelling community. They had no education. No one in authority pressured them into attending the national school, under the guise that they were under-privileged and constantly on the move.

If we, the supposedly better-off ones, stayed home from school for more than one week without a written excuse from our parents, the local Garda was on the doorstep demanding explanations, and warning about a term in jail... something that was treated very seriously in our house. He need not have worried. You couldn't get a day off school in our abode unless you were really, really ill. We tried it, but my Mother was too well versed in fact and fiction, to be hoodwinked by her own unruly bunch.

She looked forward to having a few hours of peace while we were away all day, when she could "tackle a bit o'sewin'", or similar tasks which required her undivided attention. It was gall and wormwood to us to be restricted to the school playground at lunch-time when the young tinkers rode by on the back of a cart, sticking their tongues out and boo-ing when we were in no position to retaliate. They didn't have to get cleaned up on Sundays or go to Mass. We resented this when we heard the subject discussed, but we eventually accepted it. They had no Sunday clothes, and no money to purchase such things, they maintained. One would then assume they would be grateful to the few generous people who gave them children's clothes. Occasionally, however, certain mothers among them, prickly as hedgehogs, stuffed the clothes into the bushes immediately they were out of their benefactor's sight.

The childher weren't down to wearin' "casht-offs", they claimed.

Practically all the men were good tinsmiths. They mended pots, kettles, pans, buckets and cans. Any utensil in need of repair was put aside awaiting their arrival. They could put in a new 'bottom' in minutes; a pot-mender was in place on a saucepan in seconds; a brand new bucket or can was manufactured in thirty minutes, and at the end of the day they had a 'cupla bob' in their pockets. Sadly, a trip to the pub later that night ensured there was nothing left over for the families who were mostly in need.

It was at such times that the rowdy ones in the bunch, with a tankful of porter inside their shirts, were simply spoiling for a fight. They needed no encouragement to introduce the ash-plants.... and use them, sometimes with disastrous results. The women got involved in futile efforts to save or assist their own man, and consequently they went out next morning with bulging black eyes, and swollen dark purple patches on their faces and hands. My father often talked of the time he passed by the camp-site while a full-blooded row was in session and mayhem prevailed.

"The divil'a such crackin' sthick as that crowd had goin' on above at the Watherfall", he recalled with some concern, but obviously not enough concern to report it to the Guards. No one would dream of doing such a thing. "That crowd" were left to fight their own battles in full public view, without fear of interruption from anyone.

Next day when peace was restored they all adjourned to the pub. The men held out the olive branch and stood a few pints to the women who so stoutly defended them the previous night. They rocked and rolled their way back to camp at midnight, and fighting resumed all over again.

Once, when one of those rowdies was engaged in a serious wife-beating exercise, and a passer-by yelled at him to "lave 'er alone", he paused for a second, ash plant suspended in mid-air, and blustered,

"It's all right, sir, I know to the sthroke fot she can take".

Stories were handed down from one generation to the next that the tinkers married within their own circle only, and without the customary religious ceremony so rigidly adhered to by the church. For a traditional tinker wedding nothing more ceremonial was required of the young couple other than "jump the budget" three times, or "jump the anvil" three times .... depending on the county they were residing in at that particular time. At the third jump they were pronounced married by their elders, and they hit the road together as man and wife.

It seems extraordinary now that at a time when the clergy held sway in every parish in the country, no real effort was made to integrate them into the community. We were constantly reminded at school by teachers and priests that these people were different to us, but they were still God's creatures, and as such they must be treated with charity and consideration at all times. WE had everything. THEY had nothing.

Some of us were old enough to have doubts about that. Our own mother was forever trying to fit a quart into a pint saucepan; forever re-making clothes to fit younger members of the family; forever darning and mending because she couldn't afford new garments. There was ongoing scrimping and scraping to make ends meet. She never sought help from anyone, nor was she ever in the enviable position of rejecting 'casht-offs'. Clothes were handed down from the oldest to the youngest in every home around us, until they were threadbare and torn. The few who could afford to give away clothes in our locality were, indeed, a rarity.

Cupid tried, unsuccessfully, to cross the divide between 'them' and 'us', enticing one young girl to break with tradition and venture outside the 'circle' in pursuit of love. It was a well-known fact that a certain colourful character in our neighbourhood was totally infatuated with one of the young ladies at the Waterfall. He lived alone in a neat white-washed cottage and owned a few acres of land.... enough, he felt sure, to tempt any woman. The fact that he was fifteen years older mattered not one whit, he assured himself.

"She'll be lucky to get him", the pipe-smoking fraternity decided in their wisdom. "She'll have a roof over 'er head now, fot she never had before".

Concern was expressed as to her ability to settle down and be prepared to do "th'outside work", but the young lady in question obviously didn't share their opinions or concerns. When asked if she'd consider marrying him, she replied scornfully, "I didn't stoop to that yet, sir".

****

Wily Connor didn't pine from unrequited love for very long. He soon returned to his favourite pastime... rabbit hunting. He was the bane of my mother's life once her sons were able to go "gallivanting". One by one he coaxed them away on Saturdays and Sundays for hunting sessions, accompanied by other impressionable young lads from the village, with several terriers in tow.

Connor brought his own well-trained dog, plus a ferret stuffed into a small flourbag attached to the lining of his tattered raincoat. Tough luck for the farmer who had a "carragaun" of stones or a mound of clay on his land. Connor and his workforce set to with spades and shovels, digging out deep burrows to send in the ferret in search of the terrified rabbits huddled together and completely blinded from the lights of two flashlamps.

The ferret worked swiftly and accurately, and while the young excavators never had much to show for their day's digging, apart from torn clothes, Connor certainly had enough rabbit-soup and meat to sustain him for days afterwards.

He was a familiar sight on the road to Cross where O'Mahoneys bought his rabbits for the exporters in Ballinrobe. They paid one shilling for a brace. Connor usually carried six rabbits... three tied on each handlebar of the bike, and he pedalled home, well pleased, with three shillings in his pocket.

My father had "a bit o'grazin" bought from Connor for some of his sheep, and occasionally my sister and I were sent off to count them... a dreaded task, but one we could not shirk. We closely resembled the terrified rabbits in the burrows as we crept stealthily past Connor's shed, uncomfortably aware of the ferret inside. We had strict instructions not to stop or look. If he chewed his way out he'd go for our throats and suck our blood, as the weasel was wont to do.

We were not to know the ferret was confined to his cage and released for hunting only. Freedom for him meant certain death for the hens in the village, and Connor knew better than to antagonize the women whose hens were their main source of income.

Such gory tales were designed to strike terror into the hearts of the young, although not always guaranteed to keep them out of mischief, but they served their purpose well.... for most of us. We counted the sheep hurriedly, then sprinted over the wall like beagles, in a frantic effort to put distance between ourselves and an imaginary ferret snapping at our heels, while savagely trying to reach our throats.

Home never looked so welcoming as we pelted towards it. We threw ourselves on the ground, gasping, and let the air

61

seep into our bursting lungs before we finally went indoors to catch up on our homework.

Oul' Mike who lived further up the village was another great believer in "terrorizing the gizzards in the young wans". He told the most spine-chilling stories in graphic detail. I remember interrupting him once, through sheer terror, to boast of flinging a stone at a weasel, probably because of our deep-rooted fear of those little animals. Mike pulled me towards him by wrapping the *cámóg* of his walking stick around my neck, saying,

"You're in for it, Missie. The weasel'll come back tonight, an' he'll root undher the door, an' he'll pull yer tonsils out when yer asleep". Needless to say, I never closed an eye and got three slaps next day for nodding off in class.

"A plausible rogue...and a fibber to boot". Such character assessment aptly described Connor. This work-shy little man with the peak of his cap hanging over his left ear, and his ganseys and shirts torn at the elbows, was known to all for his light-fingered tricks and his smooth talking ways. Some would say,

"He'd take the milk outta yer tay an' come back for the sugar".

When he was suspected of lifting something they said, "Ah, sure ya couldn't put it pass 'im. He's a right oul' scut", so indulgently that the word hero sprang to mind unbidden.

This was the courageous adventurer who thought nothing of going to Grants - the haunted house - at the dead of night, to hack out an antique fireplace which many knew existed, but few would dare to remove. Despite his best efforts the coveted fireplace remained immovable. Bitter defeat for the ruffian who proudly boasted that he never left anything behind. However, if he couldn't shift it, neither would anyone else. Hair-raising stuff was circulated once again about gale-force winds and apple-pelting, and savage beatings inflicted

62

by the ghosts, with dire warnings to return no more or he'd be a dead man.

An unlikely story, some thought. Nevertheless, wild horses wouldn't drag them near the place. Connor planned to resume hacking just as soon as he acquired the appropriate tools to complete the job.

He never saw his reluctant girl-friend again. She moved away from the Waterfall with the family for the winter months. Her parents pitched their tent, as usual, at Ballykine near Clonbur - not far from us - but in our young minds anyplace further than Cross seemed a million miles away.

When they returned in the spring she was no longer with them. A visibly heart-broken mother told of Kathleen's determination to try London in search of a job in a munitions factory. Familiar only with open spaces, and ignorant of the hazards of London traffic, she was knocked down by a bus crossing the street. She died instantly... two weeks into her new job.

Her mother, after rearing twenty-one children, was asked in her old age if having such a large family "on the roadside" was severe. She replied emphatically,

"Arraah, fot? Sure it wouldn't knock a fonk outta me if I had twenty-one more".

Riding Bareback: A Familiar Sight

CHAPTER 9

Christmas

Christmas was just three days away and we were anxiously awaiting school holidays. It was, undoubtedly, the most magical Christmas I have ever known. Many joyful events have come and gone in my life since then, but nothing could quite compare with the surge of adrenalin that coursed through my veins on walking into the classroom on the day we were getting the holidays, to be greeted by the sight of an enormous tree gaily decorated with tinsel and a myriad of tiny coloured candles, all burning brightly. There were balloons of all colours and shapes, and there were toys.

Nothing to write home about the young might say, but bear in mind I was ten years old, and incredible as it may seem today, I had never seen a real Christmas tree before. I was completely overwhelmed as indeed were all my classmates. My eyes fastened on a breathtakingly beautiful doll reposing beneath the tree in her gorgeous satin-lined box. Like a princess in a coffin, I thought, completely at a loss to find the correct words to describe her. How I envied the girl who would walk away with this bewitching beauty when Miss Duffy announced that prizes would be presented to the 'best' pupils in the class. That left me pretty well beyond the pale in my own humble opinion. I never felt best at anything, particularly lessons, but to my utter astonishment and absolute joy I was awarded the coveted doll... for what, I neither knew nor cared. I heard not one word that teacher spoke. I just assumed I must have been best at something. My precious doll was sitting on the desk beside me. Nothing else mattered. The fact that it was a cold bleak winter day outside was totally irrelevant. There was brilliant sunshine in my heart. The magic and the enchantment left me spellbound on that never-to-be-forgotten Christmas that has a special place in my memory forever.

Miss Duffy did trojan work the previous night to organize everything and even managed to get in ahead of us next morning to light all the candles. She didn't need to ask herself if it was worthwhile. Our bemused faces and our silence spoke volumes. For once in our lives we were speechless with the wonder of it all.

Lessons, as they were called in those days, were put on hold. We had a party instead. Nothing special, but for us it was a feast. We devoured a couple of packets of Arrowroot biscuits and Bulls Eyes in a few minutes, after which Miss Duffy encouraged everyone to sing or dance, or recite poetry - whatever they were good at.

One boy who was blessed with a marvellous voice sang "Cod Liver Oil" so realistically, doing a perfect impersonation of a weather-beaten old farmer with downcast eyes, thumping his chest as if in pain, that the teacher had him repeat it again when the Master looked in to see how the party was progressing.

> *"Oh, dochthor, oh dochthor, oh dear dochthor John,*
> *Yer cod-liver oil is so pure an' so strong,*
> *I'm afraid o' me life I'll go down in the soil,*
> *If me wife don't stop drinkin' yer cod-liver oil".*

This young lad had no mother to pack his bag and see him off to school in the mornings. He rarely took lunch with him, but on occasion when he remembered to bring something, it usually consisted of one boiled potato snatched hastily from the hens' pot on his way out the door. The older boys were aware of this, and under the pretext of playing games they pushed and shoved and knocked him around until the potato was thoroughly squashed in his jacket pocket.

Even as he sang at the party, the bullies behind him reached out stealthily and mashed the Kerr Pink, while the teacher accompanied him on the harmonium, unaware of the devilment going on behind her back. But young Mattie pretended not to notice. Nothing or no one was going to spoil this wonderful day - the day he became a Christmas celebrity.

The thought fleetingly crossed his mind that there would be no one at home to scold him about the mess in his jacket pocket. He had only vague memories of a mother dusting him down and flattening his hair with water when it refused to lie down, and his own desperate attempts to slip from her grasp.

Christmas Eve began in our house with my mother going to confession, leaving my father behind to keep an eye on her offspring. He never confessed his sins in Cross. Cong chapel was his favourite, where he met his cronies from other days, and they enjoyed a pint in Paddy Currans afterwards.

Those of us who were over seven had already got confession in school, and if by any chance we missed school on the day, my mother marched us down the road ahead of her on Christmas Eve. It was unthinkable that anyone, young or old, would be remiss in fulfilling their Christmas duties. Everyone in the parish turned out for confession and communion.

Mother usually baked currant cakes for the night. She put on a turf fire in the room - a luxury reserved for Christmas Eve only. We were allowed in there provided we refrained from jumping around on the bed. Such trust in us proved that mothers do get soft in the head during the festive season.

At best we managed one hour before the lot of us were banished to the kitchen, and subsequently to an early bed for disorderly conduct. A fight usually broke out among us and the bed was left in total disarray. Despite threats to the contrary, she never reported our misbehaviour to my father when he returned from his soul-cleansing. He would have dealt very severely with us, with scant regard for the night that was in it.

The high point of the night was Santa's visit. We never got much - just a few sweets and biscuits - but the joy of ripping open our gifts was unbeatable. We wrote and re-wrote our notes to Santa, nightly, for weeks beforehand, altering our requests in the faint hope that he just might decide to give us something different. He never did, of course, and we accepted what we got in true Christmas spirit.

Occasionally, when certain children from our school brought out their dolls and footballs and guns, a little green-eyed monster reared its ugly head - but not for long. We understood that Santa selected the nicest presents for the better-off people wherever he went. Two or three families in the neighbourhood were "richer" than we were. We reached our own conclusions, however insubstantial they might be.

How Santa managed to come down our narrow chimney we could never understand. However, all the evidence was there in the morning... soot scraped down and footprints around the fireplace where he walked around in his blackened snow-shoes. We lay awake awaiting his arrival and could actually hear him slipping and sliding on his way down, but we hid under the blankets, too excited and too scared to make the slightest sound.

We were such fanciful children really. We could "track" Santa all the way down on the thatch from the chimney and back the boreen to the neighbours' houses. His big awkward boots betrayed him. We didn't dwell too much on sleighs and reindeers then. Santa couldn't very well land in Houndswood anyway. Those things were for faraway places and of no great significance to us. His coming was so Christmassy and so magical. We were content with that.

The excitement intensified after Santa's departure and we summoned up the courage to venture to the kitchen, feeling our way in the darkness. Not that we feared Santa. We dreaded the telling-off we usually got for "wakin' up the whole house". My father quickly stemmed our enthusiasm and ordered us back to bed. Minutes later we returned, this time more subdued with the threat of a walloping hanging over us, and while my mother's patience was practically exhausted also, she always said "Lave them so. It's only for wan night".

Not the most brilliant of suggestions. We became more boisterous by the minute, and she was obliged to take down the sally rod in an effort to restore order and hope for an hours rest, before dawn.

While we loved the feel of the chapel on Christmas morning, none of us were too eager to prepare for Mass. We preferred the hustle and bustle of home, but once inside the church door the magic was working again as we gazed in silent wonder at the big red candles on the altar, decorated with sprigs of holly, loaded down with red berries. So heavenly was the atmosphere, we were convinced that God stood watching us in the long flickering shadows close to the sacristy door.

It was a pleasure to see the white and gold vestments worn by the priest for such a joyful occasion, the depressing purple of advent put aside until Lent, when penance and purple robes would once again serve as a reminder that we had to fast and pray if we hoped to enter the Kingdom of God.

Sadly, for me, it was my last magical Christmas. When school re-opened the tough guys in my class announced scornfully that Santa did not really exist. Only eejits would believe in him.

"Look 'ed ya", they sneered at me, "long string o'misery, believin' in that fella".

My young world crumbled. It felt like something precious had been snatched from me. I couldn't wait for school to end until I ran home to ask if the lads were lying. After giving the question some thought - no doubt because there were at least three more who would soon know the truth, my mother said,

"Well - yer gettin' far too big for that anymore. There's no Santa, but don't you go tellin' that to the small ones. They'll know soon enough".

Santa was no more, and sadly a little bit of me went with him that day. Farewell to a lovely young dream. He created a lot of excitement and expectancy in our house, and he unwittingly, caused many rows after his visits, but we wouldn't have swopped him for the whole world.

St. Stephen's Day was an exciting one that year. My oldest brother, then eight years, was considered old enough to go out with the "Wran". A jam-pot was washed and ready in eager anticipation days beforehand, to accommodate the 'Wran' on the great day, but panic struck when our own thatch failed to produce the coveted little bird, and young Paddy was off to the neighbours houses where the search continued with the aid of paraffin lamps until he finally shouted "I have 'im, I have 'im", with shrieks of joy.

The Wran-boys went from door to door in the surrounding villages reciting the old traditional poem;

"The Wran, the Wran, the King of all birds,
St. Stephen's Day he was caught in the furze.
Although he's small, his family is great,
Get up m'lady an' give us a trate,
An' if your trate it be the best,
I hope in Heaven yer soul 'ill rest,
Up with the kittle an' down with the pan,

An' give us a copper to bury the Wran".

Needless to say, it was coppers only. The Wran-boys never got much. One or two pence was the most they could expect in any house. They arrived home at dusk, oft times with blistered feet from ill-fitting shoes, but extremely happy counting the pennies as if they were gold-dust. Afterwards, if it was fortunate enough to survive the day, the 'Wran' was returned to its sanctuary in the thatch, where its safety and privacy were assured for another year.

To round off this memorable day, the local lads and lassies dressed up as 'Mummers' and went from house to house that night, singing and dancing. Everyone looked forward to their coming. I remember my own parents got much pleasure from identifying some of the 'Mummers' despite their best efforts to disguise themselves. My father would say "That's Mrs Mahoney's hat" or "That's Pat the Miller's jacket".

The Mummers didn't mind. They took the floor for a half-set, while the accordion player stood outside the door and let rip with *"The geese in the bog"*. Then they disappeared into the night, laughing and singing as they went, leaving a beautiful Christmassy atmosphere which we recall with infinite pleasure in the afternoon of our lives.

The Christmas Doll

CHAPTER 10

Confirmation

"**C**onfirmation will be held in this parish early in March", the parish priest announced at Sunday Mass.

"The Bishop of Tuam will confirm all eligible children from the three parish schools - Cong, Cross and The Neale - on a day to be appointed, in St. Mary's Church, Cong".

Little flurries of anxiety rippled through the congregation as he spoke. It was already the end of January and parents and teachers needed all of the following weeks to lay the foundations for such a notable event.

Preparations commenced at school immediately. The penny catechism - our faithful friend from First Communion days - was now obsolete and replaced by a six-penny "long" catechism, much too difficult to read and equally difficult to comprehend.

Confirmation was originally meant for twelve-year-olds, but bearing in mind that the Bishop visited the parish just once every three years, not only twelve-year-olds but eleven and ten-year-olds had to be confirmed also - if they were capable of reciting the catechism correctly - otherwise some of them would be leaving school, or indeed have already left, when His Lordship was due to return. The parish priest and the teachers gave the age problem their undivided attention to ensure all children received this most important sacrament. However, there was the exceptional case, when for one reason or another some young lad slipped the net at eleven or twelve, and was obliged to fulfil his duties three years later, showing tangible signs of moustache and acne.

The strong dark hairs on his legs stood up with the cold, evoking scornful sniffs among his former female classmates who thought he could have concealed such crudity on Confirmation Day.

Men, young or old, never displayed much of their anatomy in those days, other than all one could see when they rolled up their sleeves or opened their neck-band. Hairy chests were vulgar and kept hidden beneath flannel shirts, while legs were encased in Long Johns the whole year through, and few schoolgirls rarely, if ever, saw them uncovered.

Three girls from our family - one older than I, one younger, and myself - had to be togged out for the great day. My father was dispatched to Ballinrobe with a long list of written instructions for Tim in the drapery shop. The "makings" of three girls' coats was high on the agenda, and my father who had a keen eye for cloth, chose "Navy Nap" - pronounced "Navy Nab" locally - as the most suitable material for appearance and durability. We were neither pleased nor displeased, having no voice in the matter. Nevertheless, we were quite happy when my mother, exhausted from sitting long hours at her sewing machine, produced three navy coats which we wore proudly on the day we became *SOLDIERS OF CHRIST.*

An enormous amount of hard slog went into our religious studies for weeks beforehand. We knew what lay in store for us at school if we failed to answer our questions on the day. As with the concerts, all other subjects were put on hold and we ate, drank, and slept with the catechism churning in our heads. Some of us were no longer capable of concentrating for long periods, and for that we paid the price - the dreaded yellow cane was always close to teacher's elbow.

A battalion of the local Defence Force and the local Security Force marched to the Towers where the Cong, Cross and Neale roads met, to escort the Bishop and his entourage to St. Mary's Church in Cong. Parishioners turned out in large numbers, lining the roadside to welcome and get a glimpse of His Lordship, who drove through their midst obviously well pleased to have such an excellent gathering of the faithful awaiting his arrival.

Most people made sacrifices in order to participate in this ceremonial event. All outdoor work, wherever possible, was postponed until the morrow. Cows were milked at dawn. Unavoidable tasks such as feeding calves, pigs and hens were hurriedly implemented to allow enough time for the men to get spruced up, while the mothers of the parish battled with over-excited children in an effort to get them to the church on time.

Nervousness tinged with cowardice gripped us when the Bishop appeared and moved to the centre of the high altar to address his flock. He looked so severe, and in our humble opinion, so bad-humoured, that the feelings of dread increased considerably.

How could we possibly answer correctly when this aloof man questioned us? Confidence ebbed away slowly until the eleventh hour when it became clear that he would examine the twelve-year-olds only. The relief was palpable among those of us who did not belong to that category. The fact that my older sister WAS twelve did not worry me unduly. It was common knowledge that she had brains to burn, unlike me.

The rest of us were cross-examined by a priest who accompanied the Bishop - a complete stranger - a foreigner almost - in our narrow little world, whom we instantly regarded with fear and suspicion. Was it surprising that we stood before him like quivering jellies waiting for the axe to fall?

Contrary to expectation, he managed to put most of us at ease. Our replies to his questions were obviously satisfactory, and when a slight little smile touched teacher's lips, we knew we had stuttered through the most nerve-racking test of our lives.

The chapel was filled to capacity with parents and parishioners, and as each class completed their exams they were marched out into the cold damp day for a breath of air. Strict instructions were issued to keep within the vicinity of the church until everyone was called back for the actual confirmation ceremony. The "brassy lads" ignored orders and disappeared into the old ruins of the adjoining abbey with mother nature overtaking at an alarming rate. When a distraught teacher virtually despaired of their return they shuffled into their seats with hangdog expressions, smelling strongly of Woodbines.

We waited patiently for our turn to receive the sacrament of confirmation, pondering all the while on the slap in the face about to be administered by His Lordship. When that rumour had completed the rounds at school, it was no longer a "slap" but a "good hard wallop" guaranteed to leave a tingling sensation in one's jaw for hours.

The expressions on the faces of my companions, and on mine also I suspect, were almost comical when that austere man scarcely touched our cheeks - gently, softly, like a dewdrop, while he prayed devoutly that we would never, ever, renounce our faith, but remain forever *SOLDIERS OF CHRIST.*

To conclude the ceremony, he preached a short homily on all the graces and blessings, but more importantly on the extra strength bestowed on us by The Lord on our special day. Spiritual strength, as distinct from physical, he stressed, which was cold comfort for the ninety young parishioners who had to hoof it home, mentally and physically exhausted, before darkness descended on the cold bleak countryside.

It was a day of mixed emotions, tempered with the eventual sweet smell of success that had hung so precariously in the balance for hours, through lack of self-confidence and a fear of the unknown.

****

The trauma of that day was receding into the background of our memories when we were called upon to commence training once again, this time for the Liturgical Festival in Tuam. All schools were obliged to participate in this innovative Diocesan vocal contest, and our beloved Miss Duffy of our concert days was responsible for the selection and training of the group representing Cross school.

She restored our confidence as no one else could do. It was a joy to stay on after school and practice our hymn-singing until our throats ached. From the dent of repetition the hymns sunk into our minds, never to be forgotten.

They were all in Latin. We had "Salve Régina", "O Salutaris", "Tantum Ergo" and "Ave Vérum". Passages from the Ordinary of the Mass, such as "The Kyrie", "The Gloria", and "The Credo" were also included, but we had no fear. We knew we could do it.

This was all very impressive and a wonderful boost for the children in my mother's considered opinion, until she realised that not just one, but all three of her recently acclaimed *SOLDIERS OF CHRIST* were among the chosen ones.

What if more new outfits were required? She had neither the money nor the time to indulge in such luxury, but far be it from her to voice her thoughts aloud. When it became official later on that nothing more than a good singing voice was required, relief washed silently over her. Such welcome news lessened the strain considerably for the mothers of the parish. However, they still had to find pocket-money which amounted to no more than sixpence per child, but that was a tidy sum in those days of insufficient income on small farms in the west of Ireland.

Transport was arranged by the parish priest and paid for by the parents with additional donations at the church door on Sundays. It was a new and exhilarating experience for us to travel in a motor-car at that time. We resembled sardines in a tin with six of us piled on top of each other in the back seat, while two more were squeezed in beside the driver. We didn't mind the tight crush. We were gloriously happy and wished the journey could go on forever.

The adjudicator decided on "The Credo" - the longest and most difficult of them all - to test the skills of Cross school children. He listened attentively and signalled for us to stop when we reached "Et homo factus est", which disappointed us more than a little.

Nodding approval to his clerical colleagues, he jotted down some notes, gestured to Miss Duffy to lead us away, and once again we were crammed into the waiting cars that took us through frosty unfamiliar country.... and home.

****

We didn't buy much with our sixpence that day, just a small packet of Arrowroot biscuits, but we consoled ourselves with the thought that it was Lent and therefore sinful to indulge in "sweet things".

The church reminded its flock annually to fast and abstain on the days commanded. Adults over eighteen and under sixty were obliged to observe the Lenten fast unless a doctor specifically advised otherwise, or people had some equally valid excuse to salve their conscience. The rigidity of the rules and the depth of unquestioning faith were sufficient to assure the clergy that the fast would be religiously adhered to throughout the lean hungry days.

One full meal and two collations were allowed per day, while Wednesdays and Fridays were strictly meatless days. Some of the more devout churchgoers abstained on Saturdays also, as a form of extra penance, but the cynical ones in the locality saw this as a purely economic exercise. The fletch o'bacon lasted longer that way, they maintained.

Fish was in great demand during the abstention period, with herrings and ling proving most popular. That dreaded salty ling. We detested it. It swelled up into a wholesome lump from its normal flat state when it was boiled, disposing of a large amount of salt in the process.

The more discerning mothers, such as ours, occasionally made a smooth creamy sauce from white flour to accompany the ling, in an effort to whet their youngsters' appetites, sometimes unsuccessfully, but those who refused to eat it had to make-do with potatoes and butter. There were no second choices for stubborn children...

Easter Sunday compensated for the six weeks of "starvation". Eggs were traditional fare on the day, and while some children ate them until they practically threw up, such waste was never tolerated in our home. At the most we had two each, but we did have lots of home-made currant cake and jam which we relished much more than any number of eggs. We also experienced the joy of having a picnic outdoors on the extremely rare occasions when weather permitted. We sat in the shelter of the reek o'turf while the April breeze blackened our faces with turf-dust, but we wouldn't change places with the highest in the land.

On one such occasion an old woman peered over the garden wall and remarked,

"Ya hav'ta ate a ton o'dirt in yer lifetime, butcha don't hav'ta ate it all in one go".

Cong Abbey in Recent Years

CHAPTER 11

Eye-Opener

My father was usually present at the births of his children, or as we believed in our younger days, he was there when the doctor opened his black bag and took the baby out. Although we didn't realise it then, it was unheard of to have a husband present on such occasions, but obviously my father was not a man to be fazed by a little thing like childbirth. He chatted amicably with the doctor, in the bedroom, as my mother's labour progressed, despite baleful looks from Grandma which clearly suggested, "Getta blazes outta here". They retired to the kitchen then for a leisurely smoke, the doctor checking his watch continuously.

My father puffed away on his pipe, while his companion smoked Gold Flake cigarettes. The hand holding the cigarette was held to eye level with the little finger protruding conspicuously - a sure sign of great breeding. He tossed away good-sized "butts" from the cigarettes - another sign of good breeding and prosperity - before he returned to the "labour ward". Once there, he removed his jacket, donned his apron, and scrubbed his hands thoroughly with his favourite carbolic soap, in preparation for delivering the latest arrival.

It was during one of these leisurely, smoky interludes that he muttered to my father, peering at me intently from beneath his shaggy eyebrows,

"That child needs glasses, Michael. She has a bad squint in her right eye", he remarked in a barely audible tone not intended for my ears. If he thought I might be distressed by this information he was wrong. I had absolutely no idea of what a squint meant then, but I felt quite important to be singled out for attention by this great man who was obviously surrounded with a halo in our house.

Apparently my eye required immediate attention as arrangements were put in place soon afterwards for an eye-test at the doctors house at midday on a Sunday. This enabled my father to be present. He could attend his usual 11.00a.m. Mass, and then cycle to the doctor's residence just as my sister and I arrived on foot. My mother insisted on my sister's company perhaps for the very good reason that she was totally dependable, whereas I proved from past experiences to be a most unreliable timekeeper.

We were requested to sit on a bench-seat in the hallway and wait for the doctor who was still in bed following a late-night call-out. Eventually he put in an appearance and cordially invited my father to sit and talk with him while he breakfasted. His wife relented a little then and summoned my sister and I to the warmth of the kitchen where we sat like two scared rabbits, afraid to move.

The maid was preparing Sunday dinner for the family and appeared nervous and ill-at-ease. Roast duck was on the menu. The delicious cooking smells that wafted from the oven tickled our nostrils and created a gnawing hunger in the pits of our stomachs. It seemed like years since we had eaten.

We were still sitting there when the duck was pronounced "beautifully cooked". The doctor's wife held out a large plate while the maid removed the bird from the oven, but in her nervous state she missed the plate and dropped the duck on the floor. "You're too hasty, Bridget", her employer told her with a saccharine smile, while her neck and face went a bright turkey-cock red. The wrathful look flung in the doctor's direction clearly said, "It's all your fault, bringing those people into my kitchen". He interpreted that look correctly and quickly ushered us to the drawing-room where my eye-test was duly carried out after thorough washing of his hands in a big tin basin of scalding hot water, brought to the table by a very obviously distressed maid.

He used the carbolic soap lavishly, working up a huge lather until great big dollops of suds fell unheeded on the highly polished table, and all the time he never ceased talking politics with my father.

We gave graphic details of the duck's "crash landing" when we arrived home, much to my father's amusement.

"You'd want to see the 'praiseach' on the floor", he told my mother, laughing heartily, with little thought for the maid's discomfort and the scolding she almost certainly got from her furious mistress.

"Easy knowin' you don't have to cook", my mother retorted. However fond she was of the doctor and his family, she shared a certain empathy with the overworked maid-of-all-tasks in their household.

To this day, each time I visit an optician, memories come flooding back of the doctor's kitchen, and the duck lying on the flagstones with severe injuries to its back and neck.

I was in seventh heaven when I got my glasses two weeks later, but it was all very short-lived. The doctor issued instructions to remove them during mealtimes, cover my good eye and use the "bad" one only, in an effort to improve my impaired vision.

My siblings giggled helplessly while I groped through my dinner wearing a handmade eye-cover similar in shape and size to the black "diamond" people wore on their sleeve when a relative died. Mine was held in place with an elastic band around my head, which was pulled out and snapped back unmercifully by my table companions who thought it was hilarious.

Mealtimes became a nightmare. I hoped, in vain, that my mother would be compassionate and decide to scrap the eye-cover. Copious tears failed to bring about the desired results.

She monitored my progress - or lack of it - for weeks, but eventually she was obliged to ease up. There was a houseful of children younger than I clamouring for her time and attention. She just hoped that without constant vigilance I would be intelligent enough to obey the doctor's orders. I wasn't, and lived to regret it ever since.

****

It was not the only time my naiveté was regrettable. Whatever little leisure time I could snatch in the evenings was spent pirouetting in front of the looking-glass. No one at school had glasses quite so beautiful as mine, I thought vainly. Those rare spells of self-admiration eventually brought painful results. Around that particular time I first heard of rouge for extra colour on the cheeks of the Modern Miss, and I set about providing my own "special" to enhance my somewhat colourless complexion. The glasses were carefully put aside while I rubbed and rubbed both cheeks with a towel until they began to smart unbearably.

Yes, I certainly had two glowing cheeks, but I also had two angry patches the size of an old ha'penny the next morning, which annoyed my mother considerably. I was mortified going in to school. The new "sub" pounced on me like a cat who had just seen a mouse, demanding an explanation. I replied sheepishly that the towel was *too hard* when I washed my face!

"Not that hard, surely", she snapped, and then,

"Have ye no soft towels at all in ye'er house?", she enquired curiously.

"No Mam", I lied bravely, "only all *hard* ones"

I could only hope she would not pursue the "hard towel" excuse any further, as my mother would almost certainly see it as casting aspersions on her laundering abilities. It brings to mind the launching of Persil washing-powder some years later. To highlight the advantages of this superb product, the colourful green and red carton featured a brilliant-white soft garment alongside a much less white and hard-looking one, while the slogan underneath said,

"Someone's mother isn't using Persil".

Fortunately for me, the subject never arose again. Next time the teacher and my unsuspecting mother met they had more important things to discuss. Hard towels and scabby cheeks were completely forgotten. I could relax for the first time in weeks.

****

How we all wished it was the Missus' "sub" who was leaving when we discovered our beloved Miss Duffy was about to leave us forever. Nothing was said at school. We got our information from the village people who were "testing the water" to see if we minded. We *DID* mind, very much indeed, but we comforted ourselves with the thought that it might not happen for years. Therefore, it was quite a shock on the Friday when we realised this was her last day with us. She dismissed her class as usual that evening with a little smile saying,

"Make sure ye keep doing ye'r lessons".

Some of us hung around the hall until the infants teacher went in to chat with her, closing the door firmly in our faces. That did not deter us. There was a huge keyhole in the door which we availed of numerous times already. We knew exactly what to expect. Miss Duffy produced a packet of Players cigarettes, and the room was quickly shrouded in blue smoke. We were fascinated. Our elders always implied that a young woman smoking a cigarette was a hussy, or worse, and if she indulged in nail-painting occasionally she was a "gonner altogether". But we knew our Miss Duffy was none of these things. Taking turns to watch both ladies through the keyhole, we assured ourselves that smoking gave a girl a decidedly sophisticated look - so confident, so self-assured.

We would *ALL* be smokers when we grew up!

Miss Duffy did many good deeds for school and church. Thanks to her, the Sacred Heart Church in Cross had a choir for the first time in its history. Sunday Mass was enriched by the beautiful singing of the local boys and girls. She devoted her Saturday nights to rehearsals, and presided at the harmonium on Sunday mornings without any expectation of reward for her services.

A local man who always prayed outside the door on one knee, as he never quite managed to arrive in time for Mass, was heard to say when teased about his late-coming,

"Sure I don't care as long as I'm in time for a bit oo' song".

****

Miss Duffy's successor was a very tall, very thin, lifeless thirty-something woman, who appeared to be totally devoid of energy. As my father was wont to say when comparing her with her predecessor, "Sure this wan has no sap left in 'er at all". Not enough to use "the sthick" on us, obviously, as she rarely used the canes supplied so generously by the Master. At the end of her term as a "sub" they were still sitting among the copies on her table, good as new. We liked her all the more and worked better as a result.

For some unknown reason she never took lunch to school, nor did she leave the classroom during playtime, or lunch-break as it is known today. Instead she chose me to collect her lunch at her digs - a local house known as The Mill, because of its long associations with the flour mill in Cross. Needless to say, I was thrilled to be selected for this enviable task, as not only did I skip ten minutes of catechism lessons to collect the lunch on time, but that motherly soul, the miller's wife, gave me two slices of currant cake and a cup of milk every day, while she prepared Miss Snee's flask.

I got three pennies on Fridays for my weekly errand. It was my first real taste of money. Such wealth was like heady wine, and while I walked around in a daze, full-scale war erupted at home because I had three big pennies in my fist and the others had nothing. My mother solved that dilemma in her usual practical way by confiscating my "wages", to the delight of the enemy. Scalding hot tears were shed while she consoled me matter-of-factly with,

"Ye'd only spend it foolish anyway. Ye know ye can't hold money".

Useless to argue that I never had it to hold it. All I ever wanted, I sobbed, was to buy a three-penny packet of strawberry jelly and eat it in the slab. It hurt unbearably that something so tantalizingly close could be snatched from me suddenly, but months later when the Punch and Judy Show came to the school, my mother had saved up enough to get four of us in to the show, and I was pleased to have contributed, albeit under duress, to this wonderful one-off family treat.

Homeward Bound after the Eye Test

CHAPTER 12

Cuttin' An' Killin'

Tempers were frayed in more ways than one at a particular time in our house. My father constantly complained that the lambs weren't "cut", - a task set aside specifically for May Day. It was a wet and windy month and "ye'd be dhrenched to the skhin" trying to separate sheep from lambs. A sly old man in the village who never got flustered about the weather, prophesied - very correctly - "The day'll come, *astór*, when the cow'll want 'er tail". As indeed she did, when the flies swarmed around her through the unexpected June heatwave.

"Cuttin' the lambs", or castrating as it is now known, was a ghastly procedure. We watched in horror as my father systematically set out to deprive the male lambs of their "ramhood", by slitting open their scrotum with his tobacco knife and exposing their testicles. He then held the frenzied little animal aloft and actually removed the testicles with his teeth. Blood dripped from his mouth and spattered down his shirt-front while he struggled to hold his victim. When the lamb was finally released, after a liberal splash of iodine on its raw wounds, it rolled on the ground in agony for a second before making a terrified dash in search of its mother.

It was utterly barbaric, but it was the only method known to, or used by, the farmers of that time. For them, it was a perfectly ordinary annual task to be undertaken on May Day before the weather got too hot and flies became too numerous and active.

Their method of curbing over-amorous rams was almost as primitive as cuttin'. A guana-bag, pronounced "jew-anna", was tied around that lusty animal's hindquarters, firmly enclosing his "ramhood", leaving a very wet, very scalded, and totally frustrated ram looking helplessly at his female companions. He was not to know how fortunate he was. His spare parts would still be intact when the bag was removed in October for reproduction purposes. He would never suffer the humiliation of being cut like his brothers.....

Farmers also cut off the lambs' tails with a razor-sharp knife, leaving them bleeding and sore, but surprisingly, there were very few casualties. We detested that much more than the cuttin', as the tails were cooked for dinner. We could smell burning wool while we sauntered over the boreen after school. My mother would hold the chopped-off tails over the open fire to burn off the wool, then wash and dry them before frying them on the pan.

These tails were considered a delicacy, but in our humble opinion they were disgusting, greasy and tasteless.

One of my brothers delighted in sending the rest of us scurrying from the table, about to throw up, simply by inspecting "his own tail" closely, and then pushing it off his plate rudely, exclaiming,

"I know which end was covering the lamb's backside. I can see the dirt!"

For that he got a sharp leck in th'ear from my mother who warned him heatedly,

"One more word outta ye, an' ye'll get th'outside o' the door".

Apart from having a big red face, he was not unduly worried. It was gratifying to watch us struggling "to keep our tails down", as we all, himself included, hurried for the door, glad of an excuse to distance ourselves from such an unpalatable dish.

Male calves were cut in the same way as lambs, but most times the strength of two men was required to hold them down on the ground. Again we watched the whole sickening process and heard the agonized roars of the unfortunate beasts striving to escape. We were so naive then, having no knowledge of reproduction or its origins. We were never given any reason for the surgery my father carried out on that particular tender spot. "I don't know" was the standard reply to all our queries, and with that we had to be content.

In those days, most of us had reached the age of twelve, and beyond, before our more learned, more mature friends at school began to introduce us to a subject that was enlightening, exciting, unclean, and definitely taboo, all at the same time. Such a warped version of the facts of life was so shocking that I still remember thinking,

"Oh no, not *MY* parents. They'd never do a thing like that".

"An' where else d'ya think they'd get fourteen brats like ye?", scoffed the school 'know-all', when I voiced my thoughts aloud.

****

Perhaps the annual killin' of the pig was more gruesome in its own way than the cuttin' of the lambs and calves. At least they got away after a few seconds of torture, but the pig hadn't a hope. There had to be an "R" in the month before it was considered wise to attempt bacon-curing, and farmers observed that piece of wisdom strictly. Therefore, the man with the knife in his hand was in great demand from November to Christmas, when temperatures were likely to be at their lowest.

That doomed animal, screaming for dear life, was bound tightly with ropes to the floor of the cart while his head dangled over a bucket. We stared in flesh-creeping silence as my father, who was an expert at this, slit the pig's throat with the big pig-knife. Blood gushed into the bucket and while the contents increased, the screeches of the pig grew weaker until he finally made a few feeble efforts to kick his way out of his torment, and then all went very quiet.

Relief washed over us as his big fat belly gave one last quiver and lay dreadfully still. My mother comforted us with the knowledge that animals could not foresee their destiny, despite their ability to sense impending danger. Nevertheless, our sympathies lay entirely with that hapless pig.

Many times during my life I have questioned the wisdom of permitting youngsters to watch such violent scenes. It certainly had a profound effect on me. The moment I drifted off to sleep at night my father was there with the knife, about to "stick" one of my brothers. When he was hanging from the kitchen ceiling, like the pig, I usually woke up with sweat breaking out all over, too terrified to scream. Next day, when I looked at my father he seemed just like any other man, incapable of hurting anyone, and I was reassured for a while, but the moment my mother quenched the lamp and retired for the night, it started all over again. I realised with hindsight, that my mother, who was a most compassionate woman, would never have dismissed it lightly, if only I had the good sense to confide in her about those awful nightmares.

Later in the proceedings when the pig was opened, the young males in our household fought for possession of the bladder, which, after a day or two of "curing" in the smoke up the kitchen chimney, was blown up into a big football. It was too frail to last very long, even when kicked with bare feet, but it provided the lads with immense enjoyment for its duration.

Suspended by his back feet, the pig hung, head down, from our kitchen ceiling, before he was taken down for salting two nights later. That was another job that had to be properly done. The whole pig could be destroyed if the salting was not done by an expert, like my father, who seemed to do the killin' and curin' for the entire neighbourhood. He rubbed the salt in with the greatest care, not merely on the surface, but into every crevice that could be seen, and he also stuffed it into short slits made with the pig-knife on the insides of the bacon 'fletches'. The fletches were then put into a barrel in the barn and left to cure for three weeks.

My mother suffered in silence while this salting operation was in progress on the kitchen table. Very coarse salt, like hailstones, was used, and despite the "expert's" neatness, some of it got on the floor. We dragged it around on our feet, ignoring the mess we were creating, until we got a sharp reminder to go an' get the twig an' sweep up the dirt, which started a fight immediately, as none of us relished the idea of cleaning up.

When the bacon had done time in the pickle, my father removed it from the barrel and hung each fletch on the joists of the kitchen ceiling. There it remained for months - another lump disappearing each day until the last pound was eaten.

Ours was no different to any other kitchen and the smoke didn't always go up the chimney, wide as it was. A fair bit of smoke and indeed some of the finer ashes from the turf sometimes found its way on to the ceiling giving us the best of smoked bacon. It tasted delicious when it was boiled in a pot-full of white cabbage - or turnips - and eaten with lots of floury 'laughing' potatoes. A far cry from the revolting lambs tails that we all detested so much.

The fresh "*grísgíns*" or pork steaks as they are known today were quite tasty. These were sliced out during the boning and cutting of the pig, and usually two of us were sent around after school to the neighbours houses with "a few for the tay". My mother took great pride in 'makin' up the puddins', and a few 'reels' were always included with the *grísgíns* "just for a thaste". We knew from experience that the neighbours would do likewise when they killed their own pig later on.

We actually liked the house-to-house calls, as we always got something for ourselves - apples mostly - which were hand-picked in the autumn, and covered with hay in a corner of the barn. The fact that we had these at home mattered not one bit. The neighbours' fruit was much sweeter than ours.

Delivering *grísgíns* to my uncle at eight o'clock at night inevitably led to helping him with a few jobs. He trudged up and down the yard with the lantern as if it was broad daylight, feeding pigs and cattle, to ensure they had full bellies for the night.

Throughout the winter he housed a big red bull behind sturdy wooden posts at one end of the barn, and the cow was tied at the other end. I had to accompany him once to hold the lantern while he milked the cow, and was more than a little apprehensive when the bull began to stamp the ground and snort with rage, while the wooden posts creaked alarmingly as he threw his weight against them.

The cow could sense danger and became increasingly jittery, throwing suspicious looks at her barn-mate and shuffling from one foot to the other. Uncle slapped her on the rump and said, "Sthop it, will ya". The cow retaliated with a vicious kick at the bucket spilling half the milk. In my nervous state, I almost dropped the lantern, which proved too much for Uncle who yelled,

"D'ya want to put the place on fire? Howld the bloody lantern stheady will ya, or else clear off home".

While he retrieved the bucket and hit another "skhelp" on the cow to "put manners on 'er", he added irritably,

"Will you sthop looking' at that fella, an' *HE* won't look at *YOU*".

Was the bull looking at me? I had good reason to believe he was. Worse still, I felt he recognised me. I knew only too well how that brute could react. My sister and I tormented him many times in the field in Uncle's absence, goading him into charging after us while we sprinted over the high wall like greyhounds, heedless of the danger.

It was a blessed relief when Uncle finally finished milking. He dipped his cowdung-covered thumb into the frothy milk and made the Sign of the Cross on the cow's rump, shoving me towards the door as he did so.

He couldn't wait to get back to the kitchen for a good feed o' *grísgíns*, despite the late hour. Some cold potatoes left over from dinner were sliced and thrown into the sizzling fat when the *grísgíns* were cooked . Then he sat down to an enormous greasy feast that spoke volumes for his expanding well-nourished stomach.

To-days Piggies may be to-morrows Rashers

CHAPTER 13

The Brothers

Uncle's bull displayed his mastery in no small way when, at a certain time of year, my sister and I were sent off with the cow to the bull. The cow seemed to know exactly where she was going, and the bull was very obviously aware of her presence when we drove her into Uncle's yard. Both began to bawl in frenzied anticipation as the bull broke into a run, his bulky frame heaving convulsively while he tried to force his way through the iron gate. Uncle deliberately refrained from opening the gate until we were well out of sight, shooing us up to the house with a warning,

"Don't come down here until I tell ye the cow is ready to go home".

Separating the excited lovers was a dangerous task as Uncle knew only too well. He carried the graip with him at all times, having learned the lesson that a bull can be treacherous, not just at mating times, but even when he seems at his most relaxed while he grazes in the fields.

Getting the cow away from the yard usually proved difficult. She insisted on returning for reasons best known to herself. We darted out the door the moment Uncle called us, consumed with curiosity about what actually transpired in the yard in our absence, but there was nothing to see except a raging bull and a highly excited cow who objected strongly to going home. We lost an opportunity, we thought glumly, to crow loudly at school and give a 'straight from the horses mouth' version of events to our more learned peers.

Fortunately for us, the public roads were practically devoid of traffic in those days. We ran miles trying to prevent that wayward animal from pelting down every boreen along the homeward route. On such occasions, one of us was obliged to sprint across the fields to get ahead of her and turn her back. A couple of young men, and indeed their mothers, very kindly came to the rescue when the situation got out of control.

"Give a hand to the girleens", the mothers would suggest, and while we were most grateful for their help, we resented being called "girleens". After all, we would be twelve and thirteen years of age in a few weeks, and had recently become acutely aware of our developing young bodies. We sniffed contemptuously and resumed our journey, vowing whole-heartedly to defy parental orders in future, and leave the beastly duties to our young brothers who were sprouting up like mushrooms in the background.

****

The oldest lad was almost ten and trustworthy enough to go to the bog with the horse and cart. I've no doubt that the fact that the horse was one of the old reliable sleepy types influenced my father's decision to allow him to drive to the bog with two or three of us sitting behind him in the cart. We couldn't afford to idle very much once we got down to footing or re-footing the turf. Our workload was clearly outlined beforehand and we had a very impatient man to answer to if he suspected us of "swingin' the lead". However, his experienced eye assured him he had no cause to complain. He smoked his pipe in companionable silence when the days work was done, idly watching the people - who also had plots in the same bog - gather up their forks and slanes and dinner-bags, test the tyres of their bikes that were turned upside down all day in the shade behind a rick of turf, and pedal briskly to Langan's Pub in Shrule for a well-earned pint.

Once they were out of sight, he usually turned his attention to the vast almost deserted bogland in front of him, refilling his pipe in a leisurely way. Immersed in his own thoughts he seemed unaware of our presence until we began to pelt each other with clods of turf. Then he roused himself sufficiently to harness the horse and put him under the cart with his trusty son, promising to catch up with us later on his bike. We headed for home, tired but happy, with the sun setting in the west like a great big fireball.

The lads proved to be good workers and very soon they were capable of "givin' a day" to the neighbours with hay or corn on the ground. Youngsters were regarded as ideal for "makin' cockeens o' the hay" or "bindin'" oats or wheat, which was back-breaking for the farmers, but no problem for young lads, they reckoned. Not strictly true. All youngsters experienced backache for the first day or two of constant bending over, but they were considered pettish and sissyish if they complained. However, they loved working for the neighbours where they felt they were treated like adults, and if they were lucky they could find themselves with sixpence in their fist for five evenings and all day Saturday. Their chests swelled with juvenile pride. It was a fortune in the hands of the penniless, and the neighbours smiled, well pleased, knowing the lads had done the work of two or three men, and, undoubtedly, had done it just as well. The village joker, remarking on the tight-fistedness of some farmers, scoffed,

"It's like pullin' a cat out oo'sthockin' tryin' to get money outta that shower".

Nevertheless, my brothers were happy with their "wages". One day they would each be able to buy a bike, they boasted. Unfortunately, the bikes were put on the back burner for a year when someone introduced them to Woodbines, and they smoked away their meagre savings around the hearth in a neighbour's house, where the *seanachaí* gathered to swop stories of old days and old ways.

If you have ever known the cosiness of a farmhouse fireside on a cold winter night, you will appreciate the magic of sitting in front of a roaring turf fire, listening to the men outdoing each other with tales of yesteryear. Hair-raising stuff mostly, designed to put the "fear o'God into the young wans with their ears cocked". My brothers had the wind up so bad, they were reduced to begging the more spunky ones of us to come down for them at ten o'clock. They might forget the time.

There was no way they were going to forget the time. They were well aware that their visitin' was over if they disobeyed the rules, but they were too scared after a night's ghost-stories to run across the two fields separating them from home. I was one of the spunky ones sent out to remind them of the time, and with four of us sticking close together and shouting just a trifle too loudly, nothing could jump out of the bushes, we hoped.

Frightened they most certainly were, but such story-telling was always addictive despite its spine-chilling effects. They went back for more until the day they left home to make a new life in England, and they missed it more than they cared to admit for a long, long time.

The master of that house, a roguish seventy-something, burly little man, sat beside the fire with the turf-box right behind him for convenience. My brothers were fascinated, during their day-time visits, when a hen usually came into the kitchen and cautiously picked her way to the turf-box, where she laid an egg. The old man, with the egg-saucepan ready and waiting in the hob, reached into the turf-box for the egg, put it on to boil over the hot coals, and promptly ate it amidst much puffing and blowing to avoid scalding his mouth. Could a fresh egg be any fresher than that?

Fair days were exciting times also for the lads, when men came in from the hinterland with caps and long coats and ash plants, and cattle stood outside the doors in the public streets of Ballinrobe and Clonbur. It was a situation that continued for very many years until marts were introduced and built on the outskirts of the towns, to the intense relief of the townspeople, who were sick of sweeping cow-dung away from their premises when the fair was over and the last animal moved off the street. The stench of dung lingered in the shops and private houses for hours afterwards.

My brothers were much in demand for walking cattle to the fair. It could be described as running rather than walking. One particularly overweight farmer always hired them well in advance, and suggested they overnight at his house, lest they oversleep in their own home. They had a two a.m. start to reach the town before dawn, but that farmer need not have worried. The lads couldn't close an eye. He put them inside him in the big double bed and he belched and he blew as he lay on his back, hands folded across his ample chest, and the lads lay beside him giggling into the blankets while they waited for the alarm clock to go off.

They too, learned to use the ash-plant liberally to keep the cattle close together all day. No mean feat when animals were completely disorientated and ready to bolt any second. If the farmer sold and got a good price, he treated them to dinner which usually consisted of tea and bread. But if the sales were bad and the cattle had to be walked home, the lads considered themselves lucky to get a "pennerth o' bulls eyes" for chewing on the journey.

The fact that there would be no "wages" until the cattle were sold did not worry them unduly. It was payment in itself to be treated like men and given the responsibility of driving the cattle home alone, while the farmer strolled into a nearby pub to drown his sorrows and discuss the sorry state of the country with his melancholy mates. In their dejected mood it normally took a few hours and several pints of black porter to overcome their disappointment and decide that theirs was a great little nation after all.

Trudging around with the village men seemed to increase their keen sense of hearing for the lads. They picked up hackneyed phrases that they were well advised to forget.

"Ta' care would ye say that when ye go home or ye'll get a leck in th'ear", the older men warned them sternly when they realised they were eavesdropping, but the warnings oft times went unheeded, as the following story illustrates:

It was customary for my father to begin airing his grievances with, "It's a hell of a thing", when his tools were mislaid or gone missing in the barn.

"It's a hell of a thing that I can't lave anythin' outta me hands but ye have it gone", he'd say heatedly, and my brother, knowing this, beat him to it once, by quoting something he had overheard.

"It's a hell of a thing to sthrip in yer skhin, an' go to bed wit a sthranger".

The faces of those around him made him aware that he had dropped a clanger of some sort. My mother couldn't have been more shocked if he had said he had just burned down the barn.

"Where did ya hear that?" she demanded suspiciously when she could trust herself to speak.

"Ye'll sthay at home in the evenings in future if that's fot yer learnin'", she decided with grim determination and there the matter ended for her. But not for Paddy, whose curiosity was well and truly aroused. Hell-bent on exploring further, he discussed the matter with his mates at school, and delighted to show-off, they treated him to a crude and distorted lesson on the facts of life that, like his sisters, he considered to be enlightening, exciting, but on reflection, most definitely taboo.

As the brothers grew older it became the high point in their lives to go to Cross frequently and meet up with the local gang. That was in the days when gathering casually at the street corner at dusk was pivotal to Irish life in general and the village of Cross in particular. Every young man - and indeed the not-so-young from the surrounding countryside converged on Cross to swap idle gossip and get a few "smokes" for the night.

Like the storytelling, they missed it greatly when they left home, but they carried evergreen memories with them that have lived forever in their hearts.

The Brothers

CHAPTER 14

Broadening Our Horizons

Hession's Corner and outside Mike Walshe's grocery shop were the favourite places for congregating at night. Cross had a certain magnetism, not just for the lads, but for everyone who was familiar with the area.

It was a picturesque little place, with its chapel, school, three pubs, two grocery shops, post office, flour mill, and a stretch of rolling river meandering through the village on its never-ending journey to Lough Corrib.

The bridge spanning the river fascinated us, not for its beauty, but for the fact that each time we crossed it we climbed on to the wall to gaze into the deep waters below, and watch the occasional fish borne along at high speed in the tail-race flowing towards us from the mill.

There was a trouncing in store for the more courageous lads in the fifth class when they were reported for attempting to run along the parapet on each side of the bridge. They were dicing with death in an idiotic attempt at exhibitionism, but the severe hiding they got from the new schoolmaster left them in no doubt that a repeat performance would be ill-advised.

The woman who blew the whistle on them later confessed that she was terrified just watching them.

"I was shiverin' in me skhin", she declared. "In me minds eye I could see four or five coffins lined up in front o' the high altar behind in the chapel".

"Too much o' their own way they're gettin' these days", she snapped, and with all the wisdom of seventy-five years, and eleven children of her own, she added with quiet conviction,

"*A chómhairle féin do mhac Anna is ní bhfúair sé aríamh níos measa*".

The young lads at Hession's Corner were delighted that others were "in the soup", for a change. The corner-boys as they were known, usually got the blame for any improper conduct on the street, even though their night-time activities rarely stretched to anything more exciting than smoking, talking, watching the girls, playing pitch-and-toss, and the occasional game of "horseshoes".

My brothers were not interested in girls just yet. They were glad to be offered work, and following in their father's footsteps they spent many winter nights in the mill, hauling bags of grain up to the third floor, where the kiln for drying corn was situated. My sister and I made up for their shortcomings. We had reached the stage where we certainly had a lively interest in the boys. It was good to be twelve, as I was, but infinitely better to be thirteen, and a teenager, as my sister was.

The awakening period was on the horizon, and even the dreaded school-days, which were far from over, ceased to be the ordeal they once were. We dreamed dreams and made plans for the time when school would be just a memory, but if wishes could come true my sister would have wished to further her education. Sadly for her, the resources simply were not there.

Not exactly my own sentiment, but with constant motherly encouragement I managed to stay the course until I was fifteen. I did precious little studying in that extra period. My heart wasn't in it. I could think only of the day when I would walk out of school forever.

How foolhardy we can be in our youth. In later years I oft times regretted my lack of diligence when I realised that many of life's hard knocks could have been dealt with much more effectively had I been more industrious during school-days. The old adage springs to mind,

"Education is not received. It is achieved".

Our self-appointed saviour, a distant relation who resided in England for years, assured my sister and I that one day, when we were old enough, he would take both of us under his wing and find proper jobs for us, but he showed a marked reluctance to assume any responsibility when we actually came of age. We suspected that he considered us too skittish by far, and balked at the idea of being morally accountable for us while we were under his fatherly eye.

We did not allow ourselves to dwell on the subject for long. Time enough for that when we finally left school, we decided, but despite our apparent indifference, my sister, who was becoming more adventurous as freedom beckoned, felt temporarily let down. Personally, I was secretly glad he withdrew his promise. If push came to shove I knew I wouldn't move far from home. County Mayo was a massive place. I had no wish to venture beyond its boundaries.

Anyway, there were more important things in life than bungling relations, we decided dismissively. We concentrated instead on our choir practice sessions, which seemed to stretch far beyond school hours into the late evening, in preparation for replacing the original church choir who devoted so much of their time to such a worthwhile service. Some members were moving to Dublin to seek employment, while others married local farmers and soon had more pressing commitments.

We were apprehensive at first to be stepping into their shoes, but my sister, who was lead soprano, was selected to head up the new junior choir, and she led us through Benediction on Sundays with great flair and confidence.

We occupied the front seat on the gallery and were obliged to come downstairs to receive Holy Communion during Mass. The local lads always sat on the gallery steps due to lack of space in our church, and as we stepped down they grabbed our ankles and patted our backsides, giggling and whispering nonsense while we pretended a nonchalance we certainly didn't feel.

On one such occasion, a stripling among them got it all wrong. He was not to know they targeted school-girls only for their tomfoolery, and in his eagerness to join in he touched the legs of a haughty old lady as she descended majestically from the second seat on the gallery. There was concern among some, but laughter among most when she brandished her ivory cane and threatened to summon the priest. The church caretaker intervened hastily and advised against such drastic measures with much agitation. After all, if the priest had to come down and chastise those young hooligans while he was still wearing his vestments, and still distributing Holy Communion, the lot of them would drop dead right there on the stairs, and a well-bred lady such as herself wouldn't want that, would she?

Still angry and shocked, she remained on after Mass to discuss her ordeal with a learned friend, a middle-aged bachelor man who had a hang-up about undisciplined youngsters, and blamed everything they did on the impending swing away from nature's method of feeding babies.

"Sure they're firin' cows milk into *garsúns* now, the minnit they're born, so there's bound to be the nature o' the bull in them", he consoled her, as if that explained their behaviour.

Slightly mollified by such words of wisdom, she was persuaded finally, to let the matter rest. Determined, however, to have the last word, she assumed her role of Lady Muck once again and exclaimed,

"Well, he certainly failed to lower *MY* dignity", with a return of her old hauteur. Afterwards, the caretaker/steward, whose sight was not the best, had difficulty removing the desecrators from the stairs. They pelted him with balls of paper, rolled up and chewed in their mouths, to ensure a resounding smack when the wet lump hit his balding patch. The giggling was loud enough to reach the ears of the priest. He turned around with a prolonged vexatious look towards the back of the church, fully aware that "the boyo's on the stairs were at it again", and wondered, not for the first time, why Willie never perfected the art of leaving bad enough alone. He, himself, would put the fear of God into those rascals when they least expected it.

Not many prayers were said at such times, nor were any said during Lent when we tripped down to the chapel at night to make the "Stations of the Cross". Great emphasis was placed on making a station at that time, and we were encouraged both in the home and at school to fulfil our Lenten duties. It was a great opportunity for us to meet up with a couple of girls from school and discuss more interesting subjects than jotters and pencils and sums.

It was not a coincidence that the corner-boys decided to pray at the same time as we did, nor was it merely by chance that they were waiting outside the door to chase us around the grounds when our station was over. There was terrific excitement in the chase and we all finished up, breathless and laughing, out on the road at Hession's Corner. But if truth were told, it was those light-hearted encounters, rather than our Lenten prayers, that motivated us to run to the chapel every night. Parental control was tight then. We always went out with our mother's warning ringing in our ears,

"It'll be yer last night outside the door if yer not home by nine o'clock".

That gave us little more than one hour for our nightly pilgrimage, but in our own interest it was imperative that we arrive home at the appointed time.

****

We were rewarded for our punctuality with permission to attend a show on one of the rare occasions when the well-known theatrical group, "The Shannon Players", toured our part of the country with their road-show. On the night, the curtain went up to thunderous applause from the audience, as the chorus girls came bouncing on to the stage clad in skimpy red tops and white flared mini-skirts. They had a wonderful repertoire of song and dance commencing with,

"Here we are again,
Happy as can be-ee,
All good fun and
Jolly good compan-ee".

They kicked their suntan lotioned legs high in the air, revealing a generous amount of thigh, much to the disgust of the parish priest, who attended the show especially to see their latest production, the highly emotional and heartrending "East Lynne", but who was, apparently, unaware that the play was preceded by a variety show.

The choreography was brilliant, but unfortunately the P.P. didn't appreciate the fact that the footwork gave the packed house a tantalizing glimpse of figure-hugging red briefs, which were certainly not in vogue at the time. The "long-legged-elasticated-bloomers-brigade" were seated directly behind him, and devout man-of-the-cloth that he was, he felt it was his duty to give good example and lead those fine ladies away from the "House of Sin".

To his surprise, no one had any intention of leaving. Instead, they craned their necks and moved impatiently in their seats to get a better view of the stage. Plonking down his black hat on his head and filled with loathing, he marched out muttering, "I didn't come here to see that".

"Good enough for 'im. Fot brought 'im in here anaway", scoffed the lads around the door with great glee. "Mush' be the firsht time ever he saw women's knickers", they sniggered, when the P.P. was out of earshot.

That incident made the local headlines for days, with some believing "The Shannon Players" would be banished from Cong forever, but the P.P. maintained a stony silence throughout, and in time the black cloud of impending exile for the road show faded into obscurity.

As we grew older we learned that Lent was the ideal time for the country's one or two theatrical groups to "make hay while the sun shone". Dance-halls, believed by many to be occasions of sin, remained closed for dancing, with the exception of St. Patrick's Night, for the six-week period of prayer and fasting. They were rented instead to the touring companies for their plays, which were considered harmless enough until the young hussies began to display a "bit o' leg" on stage. The lads didn't have any opportunity to touch the girls at a play, the church fondly believed. Well - certainly not in the same way as when dancing!

Pressure was applied from the altar to ensure that all courting couples would give up their sinful attachments throughout the holy season of fast and abstinence. They obeyed the rules by refraining from making dates, but they also managed to meet "accidentally" while making the stations of the Cross, and brushed aside the need to confess to something that happened without their full knowledge and full consent. The fact that courting was strongly discouraged during Lent made those "accidental" encounters very sweet indeed.

Cross Chapel

CHAPTER 15

Home Sweet Home

Courting was not the only 'forbidden fruit' during the Lenten period. Marriages were not solemnized by the church at that particular time. If intending couples did not wed beforehand, they could forget about it until Easter week. Many couples opted for Shrove Tuesday, not because the bride wished to do so, but because her intended lord and master was already laying down the rules. She either "liked it or lumped it". Usually she accepted it.

There was an abundance of would-be-brides in the parish whom he could choose from, and it could be a long time before she got another proposal if she let the opportunity slip by.

She passively agreed with his suggestion that it would "be handier to get it over an' done with before the sheep sharted droppin' an' the spring-work got undher way", but in her heart lay a wistful longing to believe the heavy workload was introduced to conceal his excitement at the prospect of having her all to himself, sooner, rather than later. One old lady in our village, with everlasting memories of her youth, was fond of telling us,

"Musha, t'was hard for the bride to be goin' into a sthrange house, but t'was a lot harder notta have a right bit t'ate for six weeks. Ye'd ate the divil when yer young", she assured us, as if we didn't know that already.

Mindful of the huge quantities of food consumed in our own home for dinner, and the "cartwheels" of brown bread that were baked daily, we could only agree with her whole-heartedly, and felt a certain empathy with the hapless newly-wed, and her lean introduction to the delights of wedded bliss.

Our outings were not as severely curtailed as we feared they might be when the spartan fare was but a memory. We needed a good reason, preferably a church or school exercise, to get us out of the house at night, and it came our way unexpectedly.

Cross school was soon participating in a nationwide project, collecting and compiling ancient folklore from the oldest inhabitants in the area, and every Friday night my sister and I were encouraged to visit - with jotters in hand - a certain lady in Cross who was by far the best folklorist around. She had an incredible amount of knowledge on all subjects, stored away in her mind, and the invaluable information which she volunteered so generously was later entered in a big black book at school and recorded for posterity.

The best writers in seniors' class, my sister and her classmate, were chosen to write in that all-important black book, but within months both of them were leaving school. They had reached the age of fifteen and the Master readily admitted there was nothing more he could teach them, unless they wished to do revision for a second year, and that would merely be wasting their time.... and his.

He wished, without much hope, that their parents would find a way to send them to the convent in Ballinrobe or Headford, knowing even as he spoke that very few could afford to send their children any further than the national school. That pair deserved a chance, he reflected. They had great brains.

I moved up to seniors' class after the summer holidays, and joy of joys, I was the chosen one to continue writing our precious folklore into the black book.

"You're a very good writer", the Master told me, tweaking my ear, "even though you're a bit of a rubber-neck at times".

Rubber-neck! He called me that name in a jocular way so many times, but at that moment I couldn't care less. Hadn't he just said I was a very good writer? My self-confidence soared. I would savour those days for the rest of my life!

However, I was not above looking down my nose at the classmates who jeered me many times prior to my promotion, but our sharp-eyed schoolmaster, who could see the storm clouds gathering, moved me to a desk right under his own eagle eye while writing was in progress, thereby safeguarding the parish folklore from a "drowning tragedy" in the contents of the big crock ink-wells on the desks.

****

There was a period of great activity in our village at that same time, which took the sting out of the school hostilities and channelled everyone's interest in another direction.

The Irish Land Commission divided the lands of Ballyhall - a neighbouring farm (owned by well-off people) - among the local farmers, and the eagerly awaited day came when a team of workmen moved in to build sod fences, and construct a new road through the farm to provide access to the newly acquired holdings.

The sod fences rose from the ground speedily and smoothly, all done with spades, as machinery of any kind was unheard of then. Hours of laborious work, knapping stones, went into the filling for the new road. The men sat on the ground with a "bag-een o' straw" or hay under their backsides, and with huge stones placed securely between their legs, they broke them up with a hammer designed specifically for knapping. Not a job to look forward to on a cold frosty morning, but work hard they certainly did, and by mid-morning the man with the horse and cart was on the spot to remove the ever-increasing pile of filling in front of the knappers. They had a poet among them who penned some humorous verses in between knapping and wall building. Most of it poked light-hearted fun at the locals, and the majority accepted it in the spirit in which it was meant, but a handful felt they were portrayed insensitively and thought O'Malley, the ganger, should have kept Maye's nose to the grindstone much more rigidly.

For the people in our part of the county it was their first glimpse of sod fences, and many came on Sundays to admire such an innovative method of dividing holdings of land. Who in the name o' God had the brains to think o' such a thing, they wondered? But they wondered even more, and many, many people arrived in the village when Ned Joyce next door to us erected a glasshouse. A brand new government scheme was being introduced to farmers with a flair for market-gardening, and Ned was the ideal man in our area. People gazed in awesome wonder at the all-glass structure purposely built for growing tomatoes, a product that only a very few had sampled heretofore.

Ned was "*flaithiúil*" in that he gave five or six tomatoes to every house to "get the tashte o'them". They looked so tempting, so luscious, so colourful, we couldn't wait to sink our teeth into them. But what a disappointment! There was only one 'taker' in our house, and the contents of the sugar-bowl disappeared rapidly as a result, so determined was he to succeed where the rest of us failed miserably.

The tomato-house flourished over the years, and Ned's market-garden was a sight to behold with its abundant display of strawberries, gooseberries, blackcurrants, apples and plums, not to mention early potatoes, cabbage and onions. He worked extremely hard, and was justly rewarded for his efforts. But not always financially, as he dished out so much freebies in the early days. He derived immense pleasure from showing off his glasshouse and his garden, fully aware that they were second to none in the county. People were full of admiration and praise, and that, in Ned's humble opinion, was equally as important as the few shillin's he made on his regular trips to Headford and Galway with his skips of fruit and veg.

Little did anyone realise then that we were looking at the slowly changing face of Ireland in its embryonic stage. The Government had put on its thinking-cap at last, and the Irish Land Commission, whose brainchild it was to divide up large country estates, initiated a migration scheme mainly for Connemara and its environs, in an effort to improve the quality of life for small farmers struggling to exist on scattered little holdings. They were offered a change to Kildare or Meath which many accepted gladly, and Land Commission set about providing some essential farm equipment, such as carts and ploughs, to enable the migrants to commence spring work on arrival in the midlands.

Another neighbour of ours, of Moran's sawmill, who already had a small little business making egg-boxes for a Galway firm who exported eggs to England, secured a contract for manufacturing hand-made carts for the migrants needs, and at one stage he had five young men on his payroll.

They didn't have qualifications in those days, but their employer instinctively knew if they "had it in them". They did all the rough work outside and inside the shed, and "picked up" the carpentry trade while they served their time.

The cart-making failed to generate the same interest as the glasshouse. After all, they were looking at carts every day, and the new scheme had nothing to do with our locality. That was for people back in the mountains who would never be seen or heard of again! Whatever possessed them to move to such faraway places, we wondered. Some were homesick. They missed their little cottages and they missed the sea. One old woman described her thoughts accurately when she wrote a poem that ended with,

115

"I'd rather one cabin in Galway so fair,
Than all the fine lands in the plains of Kildare"

I was not to know then, that thirty years later, I too, would be packing my bags and heading for the midlands in search of a better life, but as the old saying goes, *sin scéal eile.*

All in all, the relocation of families to the midlands proved very successful and was extended to many parts of the country over a thirty-year period. But carts became obsolete with time. The small TVO tractor that replaced them was, by comparison, a speedy little machine, and steadily gaining favour with the migrants. Many carpenter-sheds closed their doors as a result.

The day I was fifteen and penned my final entry in the black book, I could not but dwell on the possibility that one day someone would be recounting and recording, as ancient history, the things that were ultra-modern to us then.

Despite the Land Commission's striping of big, sometimes unoccupied holdings, prospects were bleak for large families, as the farm would eventually be for one family member only - the eldest son. The brothers and sisters had no option but to "hit the road" when they left school. Most of them, however excited beforehand, were very distressed on the day they were leaving home. I well remember the tears and the heartache when my own brothers were old enough to go to England in search of work. My mother cried for days and the lads cried all the way to Galway on the first phase of that nightmare journey on the cattle-boat to Holyhead.

Hundreds of teenage girls were leaving our shores also, as England beckoned enticingly. They could pursue a career in nursing, work in an ammunition factory, or go into service in one of England's numerous big houses .... "pot-wallopin'", as it was referred to scornfully by some.

"Did'ja hear Mary Mooney's daughter is gone t'England pot-wallopin'", they'd say, enjoying the shocked expression on their listeners' faces. Little mention was made at such times of the fact that many of these "pot-wallopers" were treated with great kindness and had their own room, albeit small, and their own radio - a rare luxury indeed.

Emigration was getting uncomfortably close, particularly for me, when our parish priest surprised his parishioners at Sunday Mass with a special announcement that a knitting industry was opening at nearby Ashford and young girls were required for work.

Welcome news for my sister and I. We signed on immediately, creating much interest as we walked to and from our jobs each day. A local man remarked to my father, "Gawd Michael, I never thought I'd see the day the wimmin'd be goin' wi'the dinner-bag undher their arm".

"Happiness is doing a job you love" we are told, and I certainly loved mine.... enough to remain in Ashford Industries for the next ten years, meeting many interesting people en route, most notably the cast and crew of that unforgettable film, "The Quiet Man", which was filmed in our locality in 1951. I could scarcely believe my good fortune to have secured employment in my own place, where anxiety about leaving home became a dim and distant memory. As the song says,

"For you will always be,
Home sweet home to me,
County Mayo, you're the Heaven I call HOME".

The End

Ashford Castle